OP '93   30 —
                          G

D1617269

Merleau-Ponty's
Philosophy of Language:
Structuralism and Dialectics

Current Continental Research
is co-published by
The Center for Advanced Research in Phenomenology
and
University Press of America, Inc.

CURRENT CONTINENTAL RESEARCH 206

James M. Edie

MERLEAU-PONTY'S PHILOSOPHY OF LANGUAGE: STRUCTURALISM AND DIALECTICS

1987

Center for Advanced Research in Phenomenology
& University Press of America, Washington, D.C.

Library of Congress Cataloging-in-Publication Data

Edie, James M.
Merleau-Ponty's philosophy of language.

(Current continental research ; 206)
Includes indexes.
1. Merleau-Ponty, Maurice, 1908-1961. 2. Languages—
Philosophy—History—20th century.   I. Center for
Advanced Research in Phenomenology.   II. Title.
III. Series.
B2430.M3764E35   1987   194   87-21622
ISBN 0-8191-6636-7 (alk. paper)
ISBN 0-8191-6637-5 (pbk. : alk. paper)

All University Press of America books are produced on acid-free
paper which exceeds the minimum standards set by the National
Historical Publication and Records Commission.

To my Former Teachers

CONTENTS

INTRODUCTION

The studies which constitute this volume were written over a number of years. My interest in Merleau-Ponty goes back to my days as a graduate student at the University of Louvain. There I encountered differing opinions. There were those who said this is not at all clear, meaning the thought of Merleau-Ponty. There is Husserl, there is Hegel, there is Gestalt psychology, and there is the history of philosophy as well as just the philosophy of history in general. Merleau-Ponty confuses them all. To which one of my younger professors, who became the director of my dissertation ultimately, said: Yeah, that's all true but it's nevertheless an interesting confusion.

I have been writing on Merleau-Ponty ever since I completed my dissertation and have decided to bring the most important writings together here in one study for publication, mainly because they had been largely lost thanks to the fact that they had been published in scattered journals throughout the world, sometimes in foreign countries, and generally difficult to find.

Chapter I, "Was Merleau-Ponty a Structuralist?" was first published in *Semiotica* in 1971.

Chapter II, "The Significance of Merleau-Ponty's Philosophy of Language" was originally published in *The Journal of the History of Philosophy* in 1975.

Chapter III, in an earlier version, was originally published as "Meaning and Development of Merleau-Ponty's Concept of Structure," in *Research in Phenomenology*, Vol. 10, 1980.

Chapter IV, "Merleau-Ponty: The Triumph of Dialectics Over Structuralism," was originally published in *Man and World* in 1984.

What these papers have in common is that they all focus on Merleau-Ponty's philosophy of language, and most particularly on his interest in structuralism, but two earlier major interests undergird, precede, and condition his understanding of structuralism and they are: phenomenology and dialectics. Like all those of his generation he had, under the influence in part of Kojeve and Jean Wahl, accepted a rather existentialized interpretation of Hegel's phenomenology and adopted very early on a marked tendency to conflate (to a greater or lesser degree depending on the subject at hand) the very different phenomenologies of Hegel and Husserl. This tendency is not yet much in evidence in *The Structure of Behavior*, still under the influence of Gurwitsch and

Gestalt psychology, but it is overwhelming in *The Phenomenology of Perception.* It was not, in fact until 1949, until well after he had finished his first major works as well as *Humanism and Terror* (perhaps his most important book on the philosophy of history) that he took up the study of linguistic structuralism in earnest and for its own sake. He could have learned a good deal from the aprioristic method of Husserl's approach to the same questions in the *Fourth Investigation* but was never able to bring himself to quite understand or accept that work as I show below. Only linguistic structuralism completely changed his philosophical perspective, for about ten years, until it, too, was once again swallowed up in an even fiercer dialectic than the earlier one. This is the drama that unfolds in this short book.

In the essays below I put the writings of 1949–1959 at the center of Merleau-Ponty's reflections on structuralism and then interpret the earlier works in which we find, first of all, a Gestaltist notion of structure (in *The Structure of Behavior*) and a dialectical notion (in *The Phenomenology of Perception*) in terms of the *properly structuralist concepts* of which Merleau-Ponty was entirely innocent in these two early works.

Merleau-Ponty, it is true, abandoned (by 1959) this "structuralist" style and method of research, and developed the "ontology" of *The Visible and the Invisible.*[1] trouble with this is that we hardly know what Merleau-Ponty means by "ontology" - a word he uses rather vaguely and to which he prefers the much more metaphorical expressions: "the intersection of being," "reversibility," "chiasm," "flesh," and so on. The categories of "the visible" and "the invisible" are primary and, rather than translate them into notions which would be more clear, Merleau-Ponty *prefers* to define them only obliquely. His last study treats of the *koinos kosmos,* which is *there,* and is thus "Being." But it is the being of the side of the object which is not seen as well as that which is seen, of the experience of absence as well as presence, of possibility as of actuality, of the mind on the surface of the body and of the body in thought, of the silence of *la langue* which makes possible the expression of *la parole,* of the unconscious as well as consciousness, of essence as well as fact, of science as an ideal as well as science as already accomplished and known, of what is "not mine" and belongs to the other as well as of what is "mine" and not to be shared, etc.

Is all this (and there is, of course, a lot more) ontology? Is there some clear thought here? It would seem to this reviewer that if this plethora of metaphors and examples can be given a phenomenological sense - and they *can* - then Merleau-Ponty's thought is fully comprehensible, because it can be perfectly well clarified *within* phenomenology. But this does not seem to be what Merleau-Ponty means by "ontology" in *The Visible and the Invisible*.

I give my own answer in the pages which follow, but it is clear that it involves Merleau-Ponty's ultimately unshakeable commitment to some form of dialectic. In order to flesh this out slightly here, by way of introduction, I would like to treat of two themes not discussed in my own text below, which is devoted to language, but which were in their own ways very typical both of the method and content of Merleau-Ponty's thought, namely his attitude towards Marxism, and his attitude towards Christianity.

But before going to that, just one more word about Merleau-Ponty's style of writing philosophy. There are those fervent disciples who are willing to be generous in accepting every thesis he proposed, whether probable or improbable, provable or unprovable, or even meaningful, as something to be treated with a method of *expositio reverentialis* of the kind that Thomas Aquinas reserved for Augustine. They are willing to believe in a rectilinear progression of thought which gets better and better till a time when the author was no longer receiving enough blood to the brain. Thus if the confusing, contradictory mass of working-notes called *The Visible and the Invisible* should contradict *The Prose of the World*, for instance, the work later in time must surely be better and truer. This principle, if carried to extremes, would have us explaining Kant's *Critique of Pure Reason* in the light of the mad ravings of the *Opus Posthumum*.

Those of us who were raised in a different intellectual climate and made our way through the dangerous and murky pitfalls of "the Merleau-Ponty non-sequiturs" (as we baptized them, and which we designated as a *type* of argument), were much more argumentative. The following chapters, I trust, show that.

Already as a student I pretty much came to the conclusion that Merleau-Ponty really would have liked to be more rigorous in his arguments if he could have been but that it was simply beyond him. After all a man's greatest strength is, as Aristotle also taught, also often the source of his major fault. Merleau-Ponty's extraordinary literary talent and education as a writer, his irrepressible imagination, his gift for metaphor, his intensity, his quickness, his impatience with intermediary steps when he could already leap to the forseen conclusion militated against it.

It is not surprising, therefore, that, whenever the hidden or missing premises in an argument can be supplied, what seemed to be a faulty conclusion turns out to be sustainable. But, unfortunately, not always, and it takes time and effort to sort out those attempts which hold water from those which leak at every joint, a

task which interested him not at all. His work is magnificent in
its very audaciousness and effrontery at times; he is, in short,
one of those thinkers who is rightly labeled "head cracking."

Of all Merleau-Ponty's writings *Humanism and Terror* of 1947
gives the best discussion of (1) his conception of political and
ethical "truth" in history, and (2) his evaluation of Marxism. It
also shows the all-pervasive strength of his attachment to some
form of dialectics.

Merleau-Ponty centers his study around the Moscow Purge
Trials of 1937-1938 and their culmination in the condemnation and
execution of Nikolai Ivanovich Bukharin (1888-1938). The interest
of these trials is not exhausted in the contrasts they permit us
to draw between a political and legal system based on the "objective" (historical) concept of *pravda* (truth-justice) of a Marxist
revolutionary regime and our Western system of justice based on
the "subjective" (psychological) concept of personal responsibility and intention. It is sufficient to recall the trial of
Petain after the defeat of Germany and the triumph of the Allies
to assure ourselves that the Marxists are not the only ones to
sacrifice considerations of subjective innocence to "objective,"
historical guilt.

> There is a sort of maleficence in history: it solicits
> men, tempts them so that they believe they are moving in its
> direction, and then suddenly it unmasks itself, and events
> change and prove that there was another possibility. The men
> whom history abandons in this way and who saw themselves
> simply as accomplices suddenly find themselves the instiga-
> tors of a crime to which history had inspired them. *And they
> are unable to look for excuses or to excuse themselves from a
> part of the responsibility.*[2]

Petain did not one day decide to sell himself to Germany;
throughout the war his *intentions* were pure, to save what could be
saved of France for the future. But even if it could be proven
that he never acted out of any other motive than his country's interests, the fact of the Allied victory required an historical
reevaluation of his position; human beings, who are historically
contingent, must always judge the past in the light of the present
and that is why French justice - which in 1944 recognized that
there had always been another possibility, namely that chosen by
the heroes of the Resistance - had to find Petain guilty of
treason.

> To ask that juries. . . furnish "guarantees of impartiality" shows that one had never absolutely taken sides, because then one would know that when it is radical, an historical decision is both partial and absolute, that it can only be judged by another decision, and finally that only the Resistance had the right to punish or forgive the collaborators. . . Historical responsibility transcends the categories of liberal thought – intention and act, circumstances and will, objective and subjective. It overwhelms the individual in his acts, mingles the objective and subjective, imputes circumstances to the will; thus it substitutes for the individual as he feels himself to be a role or phantom in which he cannot recognize himself, but in which he must see himself, since that is what he was for his victims. And today, it is his victims who are right.[3]

In the *Phenomenology of Perception* and his other major works Merleau-Ponty develops in more detail what he sometimes calls "the retroactivity of truth." Whenever we discover a "truth," it necessarily appears to us as having been true all along, and we judge ourselves and our ancestors accordingly. The physics of Newton and the psychopathology of Freud – in so far as they are true – were equally true in the days of Aristotle and Aquinas, only nobody could have known it. Here we see the retroactivity of truth as "the paradox of history." Since all experience is historical and subject to the laws of temporality, the future is at each moment radically contingent, but once it enters the present it appears real and even necessary. There appears here a harsh notion of responsibility, based not on what men intended but on what they have done in the light of what happened.[4]

This "harsh notion of responsibility" was worked out with exceptional intensity and lucidity in the life and death of Bukharin, the man among all his collaborators whom Lenin had singled out as the most dedicated, intelligent, and honorable. On the one hand Bukharin was "subjectively" innocent of the charge of treason brought against him and it is clear from the record that he never renounced this perspective on himself and his acts. On the other hand, the only weapon he permitted himself in the face of his accusers was a certain irony.[5] "I plead guilty," he said, "to. . . the sum total of crimes. . . irrespective of whether or not I knew of, whether or not I took a direct part in, any particular act." "The confession of the accused," he stated, "is a medieval principle of jurisprudence," and yet he confessed his responsibility.[6]

Bukharin was a consistent Marxist to the end; he accepted the inevitable ambiguity based on the fact that his acts would necessarily be judged not only in the light of his subjective intentions – in their meaning to himself as a psychological subject – but also in the light of their meaning for others and history. "The Moscow Trials," writes Merleau-Ponty, "only make sense among revolutionaries, that is to say among men who are convinced that they are *making history* and who consequently already see the present as past and see those who hesitate as traitors."[7] Only children imagine that their lives are separable from the lives of others and that their responsibility is limited to what they themselves have done;[8] the "hard Marxist rule" requires that a man be evaluated and even evaluate himself in the light of the "objective sense" of his actions. Since history had proven him wrong, Bukharin could know and acknowledge, no less than his accusers, that he had been "objectively" guilty from the beginning. Since he believed in the truth and sanctity of the forthcoming Communist society and since he accepted the inevitably of history, he accepted his fate. A central thesis of Marxism is the "identity of the subjective and objective factors" in history,[9] and Bukharin was too good a Marxist to question the fact that "political acts are to be judged not only according to their meaning for the moral agent but according to the sense they acquire in the historical context and the dialectical phase in which such acts originate. . . there is no margin of indifferent action. . ."[10]

Because of the dialectical cast of his own thought (the single most important element for understanding Merleau-Ponty's difficult and involuted prose), it is difficult to grasp his own assessment of this aspect of Marxist theory, especially at this point in his career when he was still intellectually allied with the French Communists though already vituperated on all sides for his exposures of the failures of Russian Communism. Clearly he does not want to say that *either* a "morality of intention" *or* a morality based exclusively on the "objective meaning" of one's actions is self-sufficient. The latter, in particular, requires that there be some *one*, necessary course to history and some authoritative interpreter of this sense (such as the Church or the Party); this he clearly rejects. Moreover, there is, in his view, no appeal to "objective history" which can absolve the individual from the necessity of choosing, because even when he sees and believes that he is responding to the demands of history it is still *he* who interprets this expectation; he can never escape his personal responsibility."[11] The true nature of Bukharin's tragedy lies in the ambiguous fact that it is *one and the same man* who recognizes "that he cannot disavow the objective pattern of his actions, that he is what he is for others in the context of history," and yet who also recognizes that it is he, Bukharin, who must recognize history as history, who never betrays the inner, moral, psychological truth "that the motive of his actions constitutes [his] worth as he himself experiences it."[12] In this sense Bukharin's tragedy is not Bukharin's alone but that of all men and this is why Merleau-Ponty can write that "there is as much 'existentialism'. . . in the *Report of the Court Proceedings* at Moscow as in the works of Heidegger."[13]

The second theme we wish to take up is Merleau-Ponty's view of Marxism as a whole. Everyone will concede that this book marks the high-point of his Marxism. At the time he wrote this book he had not yet abandoned his belief that the proletariat embodied a "collective spontaneity," a "consciousness," which was the true motive force of history[14] and the corollary to this belief that Marxism provides us with *the* philosophy of history, even though its evident failure in Russia[15] presents us with some serious theoretical problems.

> The decline of proletarian humanism is not a crucial experience which invalidates the whole of Marxism. It is still valid as a critique of the present world and alternative humanisms. In this respect, at least, *it cannot be surpassed.* Even if it is incapable of shaping world history, it remains powerful enough to discredit other solutions. On close consideration, Marxism is not just any hypothesis that might be replaced tomorrow by some other. It is the simple statement of those conditions without which there would be neither any humanism, in the sense of a mutual relation between men, nor any rationality in history. In this sense Marxism is not a philosophy of history; it is *the* philosophy of history and to renounce it is to dig the grave of Reason in history. After that nothing is left but dreams and adventures. [16]

The reasons for this rather excessive and uncritical celebration of Marxism are clearly stated:

> In its essence Marxism is the idea that history has a meaning – in other words, that it is intelligible and has a direction – that it is moving towards the power of the proletariat, which, as the essential factor of production, is capable of resolving the contradictions of capitalism, of organizing a humane appropriation of nature, and, as the "universal class," is capable of transcending national and social conflicts as well as the struggle between man and man.

To be a Marxist is to believe that economic problems and cultural or human problems are a single problem and that the proletariat, as history has shaped it, holds the solution to that one problem.[17]

Marx' "theory of the proletariat" is thus, for Merleau-Ponty, the essential component of his philosophy of history;[18] when he later came to the recognition that the proletariat is not possessed of any singular "consciousness," and that even if it were, this would not necessarily be a privileged factor in historical development but just one factor among myriad others, he abandoned his "absolutist" interpretation of Marxism as *the* philosophy of history. But here we are concerned only with *this* book and we find even here a number of discussions which logically undermine the privileged position Merleau-Ponty otherwise gives to Marxism. His strong Marxist emotions cannot fully stifle the lessons of the *Phenomenology of Perception*. Even Marx admitted this history is *nothing* but the activity of men in pursuit of their ends, and that our understanding of it is always partial because we are ourselves historically situated.[19]

Even if we assume that there is, strictly speaking, a science of the past, no one has ever held that there was a science of the future. . . There are *perspectives*, but, as the word implies, this involves only a horizon of probabilities, comparable to our perceptual horizon which can, as we approach it and it becomes present to us, reveal itself to be quite different from what we were expecting.[20]

The impossibility of a "science of the future"[21] is the most fundamental obstacle to Merleau-Ponty's complete acceptance of the Marxist "theory of the proletariat" even though he does not work this out until his considerably later work, *Les aventures de la dialectique* (1955). Here he maintains his dialectical assent to and suspicions of the Marxist theory of history uneasily together without choosing between them. After all, he observes, the possibility that "the human condition may be such that it has no happy solution"[22] is a problem which has troubled the European mind since the time of the Greeks at least. Unlike a geometrical problem, or a problem in physics, an historical problem is not one which has a fully determinate and fixed (even if still unknown) answer which we set out to discover. "One does not become a revolutionary through science but out of indignation."[23] Experience shows us only "situated consciousness."[24] In fact if one truly understands the nature of "historical dialectic," one will see that there is no possibility of comprehending the course of history in a single idea or as necessarily going in a determinate and comprehensible direction.[25] History does not guarantee the triumph of morality (as the study of Bukharin"s trial illustrates) and, having admitted this, Merleau-Ponty's attempts to explain himself in strictly Marxist terms all the same, may have to be judged as forced and unconvincing.[26] But my point is that his dialectical thrust is never lost for a minute.

As is well known after 1950 Merleau-Ponty began little by little to lose his "absolutist" faith in Marxism, in the hypostatization of the proletariat, even in its historical force, as unhistorical and unrealistic. Much the same thing befell his religious philosophy in so far as he had one. The surest guide we have here is Albert Rabil[27] since almost nobody else has ever written about it. Very early Merleau-Ponty had been influenced by Catholicism and somewhat, though superficially, by the writings of Marcel. His very first journal article was for the Catholic *La Vie Intellectuelle* in 1935, and he was still involved in it, as Sartre tells us, at the Ecole Normale.

Merleau-Ponty's change of heart on the subject of religion can be neatly illustrated by two statements. When he was asked about his "atheism" at the Rencontres Internationales in Geneva in 1951, he answered that he only used this term when he was provoked by an adversary: "I do not pass my time saying that I am atheist, because this is not an occupation and *it would be to transform into a negation an effort of wholly positive philosophical consciousness*. But in the final analysis if one asks me whether or not I am an atheist, I reply *yes*."[28] Two years later, in his inaugural address at the College de France, he intimated that one would miss the sense of his philosophy altogether if one defined it as atheism ("This is philosophy as it is seen by the theologian"). This change of emphasis thus coincides with the period (1950-1955) when, according to Rabil, Merleau-Ponty was redefining his philosophy. He had, as a young student, rejected Christianity (at the same time that he had embraced Marxism) on moral grounds. Atheism as such was never central to his philosophical program, as it was for Sartre and Camus for instance, but grew out of his ethical indignation at the immorality of the Church as an institution. Ultimately, as Rabil points out, he came to reject Marxism for the same reasons he had rejected Christianity: namely because of the irreconcilable divergence between their stated ideals and their institu-tionalized forms.

In his writings prior to the early 1950's Merleau-Ponty took an attitude towards Christianity (using the Roman Catholic Church in France as his paradigm) which was based on a twofold "theological typology." There is in Christian history, on the one hand, the conservative tradition of the "interior God" of faith, the "religion of the Father," who can be found by turning within, who is not mixed up with the world of social and political institutions but who judges them from above. On the other hand, there is the "religion of the Son," of the God who needs man and history and who enters the world through the Incarnation; he is an intersubjective and social force. The paradox of Christianity, according to Merleau-Ponty, is that it does not follow either the religion of the Father or that of the Son to its logical conclusion, but adopts an ambivalent attitude towards both. Rabil summarizes Merleau-Ponty's argument:

> With respect to the religion of the Father, for example, Catholicism does not want to give everything over to Christian faith, for it requires in the *Syllabus of Errors* that one affirm the possibility of proving God's existence by reason, but censures those like the modernists who have attempted to transcribe their religious experience of God into intelligible terms. In other words, Catholicism hesitates to say that the God who can be proved is the God who is involved in human existence. This same ambivalence is evident in relation to the Incarnation. The meaning of the Incarnation, as attested by the experience of Pentecost, is that Christ is always with us. However, this lesson was never fully learned, as we can see in the efforts of the Crusaders to locate the empty tomb.[29]

Like the medieval heretic, Joachim of Flora, Merleau-Ponty argues at this period that the religion of the Father should have been *replaced* by the religion of the Son, and that of the Son by the religion of the Spirit. It is what God is in relation to human existence that is of sole importance. As a result of its ambivalence, the Church has not historically become a part of human society but has crystalized on the margins of the state, on the periphery of the social and political world. The "religion of the Father" is potentially conservative and the "religion of the Son" is potentially revolutionary but the Christian religion is neither the one nor the other because the Christian remains "in the margins of society."

> He may support the status quo (if it protects institutional religion) or he may support the rebellion (if it looks as if it might succeed). *But as a Christian* he will neither defend the status quo completely nor help to bring about a revolution. Thus he disquiets everyone; neither the esta-

blished powers nor the revolutionaries feel that the Christian is really on their side.[30]

Merleau-Ponty is thus saying that the Christian's relationship to society is necessarily equivocal, and this is the basis of his negative criticism. In his inaugural address of 1953 Merleau-Ponty paints the very same picture for a second time, but this time it is the philosopher himself who is the one who is "on the margins," who participates in society "at a distance," and the one of whom nobody an be sure. In his rejection of institutionalized forms of Marxism, while holding to the ideal "truth" of Marxism as a valid human choice, Merleau-Ponty came to recognize that the position of the Christian vis-a-vis the Church was not essentially different from the position of the philosopher vis-a-vis his society. He was forced to conclude, after 1950, that there is rightly no "pure" Christian choice just as there is no "pure" Marxist choice, and no "pure" choice within any other framework of thought and action. To require that we act unambiguously, that we rid ourselves of all equivocation, is to demand that we cease to be involved in existence.[31] When he had said earlier (in *The Primacy of Perception*) that it is proper to man to think God, though this does not in any way prove that God exists, he had meant that God as a transcendent being could never be more than a hypothetical postulate of pure reason, an absolute thinker of the world utterly foreign to human experience; and he implied that the only possible *authentic* Christian choice would be in favor of the "religion of immanence," of God as he is to be found in human experience. But in his final writings on religion he no longer requires that the Christian, in order to be authentic, opt for either the religion of the Father or the Son, but rather that he assume within himself this conflict between transcendence and immanence which we find in all religious history and religious experience. This is, finally, a necessary equivocation whose final "truth," like all truth, cannot be seen with univocal clarity in the present but must appeal to a future dialectical reconciliation. And this means the triumph of dialectics and, as this book will show, the ultimate defeat of structuralism.

I wish finally to thank our Departmental Secretary, Audrey G. Thiel, for her work in preparing this manuscript for publication, as well as Marina Pianu Rosiene for revising it the final time.

James M. Edie
August 16, 1986

WAS MERLEAU-PONTY

A STRUCTURALIST?

It is now becoming fairly common among both phenomenologists and Wittgensteinians to look on linguistics as the newest, the best, and perhaps the *only* authentic model of what a human science can and should be – a "human" science being defined as one that gives a systematically complete explanation of some delimited area of human behavior methodologically distinguishable from the sciences (and the scientific methods) concerned with explaining "physical" or infrahuman (i.e., not *specifically* human) nature. Thus *linguistic structuralism*, which in the work of Saussure and his now myriad followers served as the foundation of modern scientific linguistics, is more and more being found to have epistemological and even ontological implications for the philosophy of man and the philosophy of science that are of greater importance than would normally be the case for just *any* newly developed scientific hypothesis or method. Among the philosophers who were the first to recognize and attempt to assess the importance of these implications was Merleau-Ponty, the first of the phenomenologists of language to take account of linguistic structuralism. Husserl himself was almost totally innocent of scientific linguistics, though it can certainly be argued that his contributions to the philosophy of language are and remain of greater contemporary interest than Merleau-Ponty's hasty attempt to reinterpret them would lead his readers to believe.[1] It is evident that other major phenomenologists, like Heidegger and Sartre for instance, are equally innocent of scientific linguistics, and it is safe to say that phenomenologists on the whole (and particularly the Heideggerian existentialists) have remained uninterested in these developments except and to the extent that, primarily in this country, they have found themselves arguing points of the philosophy of language with Wittgensteinians.[2]

In France, however, where Structuralism has now become a generalized theory, even a "philosophy," which has gone far beyond its origins in the structural linguistics of Saussure, and is being applied in almost all the human sciences, phenomenologists have not been permitted to ignore its claims and, indeed, have found themselves in danger of being displaced in the affections of the young and the avant-garde by the Structuralists who now have them on the defensive.³

Thus, from the point of view of the philosophy of language, Merleau-Ponty holds a unique place in contemporary phenomenology; he is about the only phenomenologist whom the Structuralists are wont to treat with respect and whose authority and support they readily invoke. ⁴

Was Merleau-Ponty, then, a structuralist? In order to answer this question we must first make some preliminary observations and then examine Merleau-Ponty's philosophy of language as a whole. As all his readers know, Merleau-Ponty is one of the most "dialectical" thinkers in the whole history of philosophy; he introduced into phenomenology a style that Husserl, for one, would have found incredible: he is, *consciously*, never simply on one side or the other of any given question but always, from his chosen point of view, on both sides at once. Readers with "linear" minds constantly get confused; they read along in *Phenomenology of Perception*, nodding their heads in agreement with the soundness of the argument, only to discover to their dismay, a few pages later, that this was the position Merleau-Ponty meant to destroy. He always puts *himself* into an argument and presents it in its most appealing and forceful form. There is nothing relaxed about his style; it is tense and taut. Reading his major works is much like reading Wittgenstein's *Philosophical Investigations*; it takes time and effort to distinguish the interlocutor from the philosopher, and it takes considerable agility of mind to hold onto all the threads at once so as to avoid being misled into confusing the position he means to defeat with the theses he is attempting to propound. This dialectical style, more than anything else, has led Merleau-Ponty's expositors and detractors into confusion; very few philosophers are cited so frequently as holding theses they would have disowned.

No oppositions were too extreme for his attempts at dialectical reconciliation: Descartes, the philosopher of the *cogito* and of subjectivity, can be seen in his eyes to be making the same points as Marx, the objectivist, or Freud, the philosopher of the unconscious. The structure of *Phenomenology of Perception* is indicative of Merleau-Ponty's style at its best, though this style is maintained in full force through his posthumous work, *The Visible and the Invisible*. In chapter after chapter we begin with well-argued statements on attention, on sense-data, on memory, the structures of perception, etc. from two or more of the most opposed points of view, from intellectualism and empiricism, from idealism and realism, from naturalism and subjectivism, only to find that both of the opposed possibilities are in error, and,

what is more important, *are in error for the same reason.* When we
have discovered the central point at which explanations of the
same phenomenon diverge while at the same time *admitting the same
phenomenal facts*, at that central point that must be incorporated
into each of the opposing systems but that can always be ambi-
guously expressed, i.e., can seemingly be equally well accounted
for in the language of intellectualism or the language of empiricism, or whatever, we have reached the point from which we will be
able to start again and to finally account not only for the way
things really are in our experience but also for the errors of the
opposing explanations. The truth is never wholly to be found on
either side, particularly when both involve long traditions in
philosophy whose arguments have been reworked and refined sometimes for generations and centuries, but somewhere else, namely at
a point from which all these opposed accounts can be seen to be
ambiguous with respect to the primary explicandum and capable of
being absorbed, dialectically, into a new perspective that will do
justice to both. Merleau-Ponty worked hard to earn his title as
the philosopher of ambiguity, and this should never be overlooked
in any exposition of his thought. We need not claim that he was
always successful in his dialectical resolutions, or even that he
fully justified his own method or his own style, to be fully aware
of the nature of our task when we attempt to state his arguments
and conclusions in a faithful and properly nuanced manner.

Thus to the question, *Is Merleau-Ponty a structuralist?* the
answer we should expect is that he is neither a pure structuralist
nor a pure phenomenologist (if these are properly opposable categories, as the Structuralists themselves do not for a minute
doubt) but something else, a Merleau-Pontean.

Having issued this first, general caveat, whose importance
will become clear as we proceed, let us turn to Merleau-Ponty's
philosophy of language. His writings on language can be divided
into three periods. It is true that in the Third Chapter below I
distinguish *four* periods; I do this by distinguishing the Gestaltist method used almost exclusively in *The Structure of Behavior*
from all the following works. Merleau-Ponty himself did not make
and was unaware of this distinction but I think it is a good and
correct one to make from our point of view, and I do so in giving
a more general overview. But here I am interested mainly in the
breakthrough to structuralism proper out of a dialectical phenomenology. The *first period* reaches its culmination in the chapter
on "The Body as Expression and Speech" in *Phenomenology of Perception*. In these early works the study of language is only an ad-
junct to his development of "the primacy of perception", i.e., the
thesis that among the various phenomenologically distinguishable

modalities of experience, the structures of perception are the most fundamental and paradigmatic whose analogues or derived equivalents reappear at all the other levels. From this point of view language is important only as an example or an illustration of a more general thesis concerning the origin of meaning and value within the texture of experience. Language, as a system of words that make up our vocabulary and our syntax, is one of the "stores", one of the "sedimentations", of the multitudinous acts of meaning through which men, through time and conjointly with one another, give to nature a human signification; language gives us not nature as it is *in itself*, but the "world according to man." [5] Acts of speaking must, thus, be inserted into the framework of the more funadmental prelinguistic and nonlinguistic behaviors that constitute – emanating from the experiencer – the articulations of the experienced world. Perception, gesticulation, the dance, the chant, which precede and accompany speaking, produce an actively preconstituted world whose contents and articulations can then be named and "thought" in language. Words, Merleau-Ponty says, are continuous with the primordial acts of giving meaning to things, which the human body accomplishes in its active, motile, affective perceivings of objects. Words, in short, are gestures.

> The spoken word is a genuine gesture, and it contains its meaning in the same way as the gesture contains its. . . . The linguistic gesture, like all the rest, delineates its own meaning. . . . The phonetic "gesture" brings about, both for the speaking subject and for his hearers, a certain modulation of experience, exactly as a pattern of my bodily behavior endows the objects around me with a certain significance both for me and for others. The meaning of a gesture is not contained in it like some physical or physiological phenomenon. The meaning of a word is not contained in the word as a sound. But the human body is defined in terms of its property of appropriating, in an indefinite series of discontinuous acts, meaningful configurations which transcend and transfigure its natural powers. . . . Here and there a system of definite powers is suddenly thrown out of kilter, broken up and reorganized under a new law unknown to the subject or to the external witness, and one which reveals itself to them at the very moment at which the process occurs. For example, the knitting of the brows intended, according to Darwin, to protect the eye from the sun, or the narrowing of the eyes to enable one to see sharply, become component parts of the human act of meditation, and convey this to an observer. Language, in its turn, presents no

different a problem: a contraction of the throat, a sibilant
emission of air between the tongue and teeth, a certain way
of bringing the body into play suddenly allows itself to be
invested with a *figurative sense* which is conveyed outside
us. This is neither more nor less miraculous than the emergence of love from desire, or that of gesture from the un-
coordinated movements of infancy. For the miracle to come
about, phonetic "gesticulation" must use an alphabet of already acquired meanings, the word-gesture must be performed
in a certain setting common to the speakers, just as the
comprehension of other gestures presupposes a perceived world
common to all. . . .[6]

One cannot, of course, do justice to Merleau-Ponty's theory of
language, even in this first period of his thought, with this
summary quotation. Though his thought moves along the same lines
as that of Heidegger and the German existentialists, his theory is
much more comprehensive, much better illustrated, much more tho-
roughly grounded in the scientific and philosophical literature,
and above all much richer in detail and in its implications than
the various phenomenological theories that preceded it. We shall
attempt to allude to some of these ramifications in the course of
this study. But here we must insist on just one thing in Merleau-
Ponty's early examination of the phenomenon of speech. His entire
study is centered almost exclusively on *one* of the capital
functions of speech, namely, the manner in which an act of expression enables the speaker to tear forth from a hitherto undif-
ferentiated field of experience a new meaning, and to fix it in
the intersubjective mental space of his linguistic (and cultural)
community as a common possession by giving it a name, by producing
its *word.*

> The spoken word is a gesture, and its meaning, a
> world. . . . It is impossible to draw up an inventory of this
> irrational power which creates meanings and conveys them.
> Speech is merely one particular case of it.[7]

Merleau-Ponty's concern is to analyze the structurization and
restructurization that language introduces into our experience of
the world. He is, at this period, hardly aware of the other aspects and functions of language, of the unconscious syntactic
systems, for instance, which the act of speaking logically presupposes; he is concerned primarily with a philosophy of "the
Word" (*la parole*) both in its active sense as the productive
speech ("the acts of speaking") that expresses and fixes meanings,

and in the passive sense that "the Word", once expressed, possesses as a "sedimentation" of meaning, which has now been "insti-
tuted", through language, as an intersubjective and cultural object. As in the writings of other existentialists (notably,
Heidegger) the accent is always on the emergence, the properties,
the *institution*, the meaning-structures of "words", while
questions of syntax and semantics (which primarily preoccupied a
Husserl, for instance) are left out of consideration.

It was in what we here distinguish as his *second period* that
Merleau-Ponty developed a new and different attitude toward
language, under the influence of his reading of Saussure and
scientific linguistics. Language begins to become his central
preoccupation; it is no longer treated as just one example among
many of the specifically human institution of meaning, but becomes, somewhat in the manner of Wittgenstein, but of course
without knowledge of him, the privileged model of the whole of our
experience of meaning. From being a peripheral, though always
essential, consideration in his phenomenological program, the
analysis of language now begins to take the central place. Though
he never went so far as to claim that the study of language, alone
and of itself, would enable us to solve all philosophical problems, he did make "linguistics" the paradigm model on the basis
of which we would be able to elaborate a theory of the "human"
sciences and thus establish a universal, philosophical anthropology.

His writings on language in this period are many; the
following, listed in chronological order, are the most important:
(1) *Langage et communication* (1948)[8], (2) "La conscience et l'acquisition du langage" (1949),[9] (3) "Les sciences de l'homme et la
phenomenologie" (1951),[10] (4) "Sur la phenomenologie du langage"
(1951),[11] (5) "Le philosophe et la sociologie" (1951),[12] (6) "Le
langage indirect et les voix du silence" (1952),[13] (7) "un inedit
de Maurice Merleau-Ponty" (1953),[14] (8) *L'Eloge de la philosophie*
(1953),[15] (9) "Le monde sensible et le monde de l'expression"
(1953),[16] (10) "Recherches sur l'usage litteraire du langage"
(1953),[17] (11) "Le problème de la parole" (1954),[18] (12) "De Mauss
à Claude Levi-Strauss" (1959).[19] Finally, by 1953 he had half
completed what was to have been his major, comprehensive treatise
on the philosophy of language, *The Prose of the World*, and then,
sometime around but not later than 1959 inexplicably abandoned it
and left it unpublished ending, like an unfinished painting at
Pompeii or a sign at the Roanoake Colony, with only the hint of
his chapter on structuralism and the algorithmic nature of
language.[20]

Thirdly and lastly we must mention the discussions of language that occur in his final, posthumously published work, *The Visible and the Invisible*,[21] because it introduces a shift in perspective. It no longer isolates the phenomenon of language as something to be studied in and for itself, but attempts to come to a systematic (and always "dialectical") understanding of the place of language in a completed phenomenology of the experienced world. Thus, the final work attempts to integrate the lessons of Merleau-Ponty's excursus into structural linguistics into the broader framework of a phenomenology of experience as a whole toward which he was working at the time of his death. We should, therefore, treat his third period as a footnote to the second, its dialectical reinterpretation. This will be discussed further in Chapter Three and Four below.

It is, then, in what we can (from the perspective of his philosophy of language) call his second or *middle period* that Merleau-Ponty was primarily concerned with structuralism and developing his own attitude towards it. And it is necessary to remark at once, from the beginning, that he interprets Saussure very much to his own purposes.[22]

Since we clearly cannot expound and criticize the whole of Merleau-Ponty's philosophy of language in complete detail here, the following discussion will be centered around three of the major problems that emerge from his interpretation of structural linguistics in its importance for a phenomenology of language: (1) The relation of the speech act (*la parole*) to the synchronic system or structure that renders it possible (*la langue*), (2) the relation of words to syntax, and (3) the problem of grammatical (and other linguistic) universals. And even in this we cannot possibly give a complete account of all the problems involved but must limit ourselves to three central paradoxes arising from Merleau-Ponty's "dialectical" attempt to reconcile phenomenology and structuralism in a theory of speech that will do justice to both without conceding the right completely to either.

1. THE SIGN OR THE WORD

In recent French Structuralism, as in classical linguistic structuralism, there has grown up a more or less standard, though very vague, sense in which the distinction Saussure inaugurated between *la parole* and *la langue* is to be understood, and this has now been extended to cover all the recent structuralisms that have followed upon it insofar as these various "sciences" deal with subliminal, unconscious, or preunderstood structures that can be related to surface experience as Saussure related *la langue* to *la parole*.

Saussure distinguished *la parole*, i.e., the actual experience of speaking, the speech act, from *la langue*, i.e., the system of phonological rules that permits the construction of words in a given language through the distinctive, oppositive sounds. He devoted an entire chapter of his famous *Cours de linguistique generale* to arguing that *la langue* is the unique object of study for linguistics and that *la parole*, though not without significance in itself, falls outside the purview of scientific linguistics. For a scientific study of language it is *la langue* that is, he says, "the essential", whereas *la parole* is "the accessory" or accidental.[23] Structuralism, which is based on a generalization of this distinction, can easily appear to be nothing other than a new and more sophisticated (i.e., French) version of positivism. Since the direct study of consciousness, of historical origins, of functions and processes, of the individual act itself, the existentially real and concrete experience, leads us into the realm of the subjective, the unique, the non-repeatable, the uncontrollable irruptions of free choice, which can be neither predicted nor accounted for *in theory*, Structuralism directs its "scientific" attention toward the analysis of the macroscopic and intersubjective structures, the statistical regularities, the nontemporal and nonparticular *synchronic* forms to which behavior can be found to conform. In psychiatry, individual experience is replaced by the study of the structures of an unconscious that, we are told by Jacques Lacan, is structured like language. In anthropology, sociology, linguistics, and other human sciences the focus is shifted away from the study of man as the subject of experience, as the *cogito* in whom and for whom the world is constituted as meaningful, toward the objective structures of thought (and language). It is no longer a study of man who thinks or speaks but of the language that speaks in and through him. It is not that individual experience or consciousness is denied, but rather that the focus is shifted away from the "heroic" vision of man as the source and creator of his own history and of his social institutions to the supposedly infrahuman and "automatic" rules governing his behavior. Attempts to account for the structure of thought either by accounting for its historical genesis through a diachronic study of the processes of its development, or for its transcendental conditions through the logical analysis of the contents of consciousness *as such*, are abandoned in favor of a purely descriptive, nonhistorical, *synchronic*, study of its objectified forms. The methods of Kant and Husserl, no less than those of Hegel and Dilthey, are to be completely bypassed.

There is, of course, in attempting to characterize a style of thought that embraces as many disciplines as does contemporary Structuralism, the danger of becoming altogether too vague. Merleau-Ponty warns of this in his discussion of Levi-Strauss, where he also succinctly gives his own understanding of the term "structure" in the sense we will be using it throughout this essay:

> Social facts are neither things nor ideas; they are structures. Overused today, this term had a precise meaning to begin with. . . . In linguistics. . .structure is a concrete, incarnate system. When Saussure used to say that linguistic signs are diacritical – they function only through their differences, through a certain spread between themselves and other signs and not, to begin with, by evoking a positive signification – he was making us see the unity which lies beneath a language's explicit signification, a systematization which is achieved in a language before its conceptual principle is known. For social anthropology, society is composed of systems of this type. . . . The subjects living in a society do not necessarily know about the principle of exchange which governs them, any more than the speaking subject needs to go through a linguistic analysis of his language in order to speak. They ordinarily make use of the structure as a matter of course. Rather than their possessing it, it possess them.[24]

If one were to take Merleau-Ponty's numerous professions of discipleship to Saussure at face value, one would say that he begins with a total acceptance of Saussure's semiology. His interpretation of this semiology enables him to bring his earlier reflections on speech as linguistic gesticulation together with Saussure's theory of the linguistic sign and to interpret Saussure philosophically:

> What we have learned from Saussure is that, taken singly, signs do not signify anything, and that each one of them does not so much express a meaning as mark a divergence of meaning between itself and other signs.[25]

> The well-known definition of the sign as "diacritical, oppositive, and negative" means that the language is present in the speaking subject as a system of intervals between signs and significations, and that, as a unity, the act of

speech simultaneously operates the differentiation of these two orders.[26]

Prior to Saussure, it was usual to define the word-sound (what he calls the "acoustic image") as the *sign* (*signifiant*) of its meaning or of its reference. Thus the sound of the word "tree" would evoke, because of a conventional association, the concept (*signifie*) and, through the concept, the actual individuals of the class of beings called "trees. The earlier semiologies, which went back to Aristotle and Ockham, made no essential semiological distinction between so-called "natural" signs (smoke as the sign of fire) and "linguistic" signs. In opposition to the tradition that treated all signs as belonging to the same genus, Saussure based his semiology on the recognition that, in language, the interpenetration of the *signifiant* by the *signifie* does not permit this artificial separation of the one from the other. The word-sound does not, *merely remind* us of the idea with which it is associated. Saussure thus gives the linguistic *sign* a technical sense; he reserves the word *sign* to designate the *combination* of the concept (*signifie*) and the acoustic image (*signifiant*) into a unity. "We propose", he wrote, "to keep the word *sign* to designate the totality [i.e., the word as meaningful] and to replace the words *concept* and *acoustic image* by *signifie* and *signifiant* respectively."[27]

Even before he took up Saussure, Merleau-Ponty had already suggested that the relation of the word-sound to *its* meaning could not be purely "conventional". This sounds paradoxical. On the one hand the very existence of a plurality of different languages in which we can all speak of the same things differently seems to point to some kind of "natural convention" thanks to which, in a given language, certain phonemic patterns are paired with certain meanings. But, on the other hand, we recognize that "conventions are a late form of relationship between men" and that the different groups of languages cannot have arisen through any explicit grasp of the rules according to which sounds and meanings are to be paired. This is "an unknown law", and in *Phenomenology of Perception*, Merleau-Ponty goes so far as to formulate the following unverified, and probably unverifiable, hypothesis:

If we consider only the conceptual and delimiting meaning of words, it is true that the verbal form . . . appears arbitrary. But it would no longer appear so if we took into account the emotional content of the word, which we have called above its "gestural" sense, which is all-important for poetry, for example. It would then be found that the

words, vowels and phonemes are so many ways of "singing" the
world, and that their function is to represent things not, as
the naive onomatopoeic theory had it, by reason of an objective resemblance, but because they extract, and literally
express, their emotional essence. If it were possible, in any
vocabulary, to disregard what is attributable to the mechani-
cal laws of phonetics, to the influence of other languages,
the rationalization of grammarians, the assimilatory processes, we should probably discover in the original form of
each language a somewhat restricted system of expression, but
such as would make it not entirely arbitrary to call night by
the word *nuit* if we use *lumiere* for light. The predominance
of vowels in one language, or of consonants in another, and
constructional and syntactical systems, do not represent so
many arbitrary conventions for the expressions of one and the
same idea, but several ways for the human body to sing the
world's praises and in the last resort to live it. Hence the
full meaning of a language is never translatable into another. We may speak several languages, but one of them always
remains the one in which we live. In order completely to
assimilate a language, it would be necessary to make the
world which it expresses one's own, and one never does belong
to two worlds at once. . . . Strictly speaking, therefore,
there are no conventional signs. . . .[28]

If we are properly attuned to the dialectical cast of this thought
and style, it is not necessary to attempt an empirical validation
or refutation of this statement by examining cases of bilingualism, as was suggested, for instance by Alphonse De Waelhens –
who rightly challenged Merleau-Ponty on this point on the sound
basis of his own perfect bilingualism.[29] As always, Merleau-Ponty
is bringing into the clearest opposition possible two theoretically possible viewpoints on the phenomenon of language neither of
which is *exclusively* true, namely that different languages can
speak of the *same things* in different phonemic patterns, following
different phonological rules, while at the same time there remains
beneath the level of what these patterned sounds enable one to
think conceptually, an untranslatable, primitive level of meaning
distinctive of that language and expressive of its primordial
melody, intonation and poetic "chant". And it is the latter fact
that is at least chronologically and existentially prior to the
former. For the speakers of a given language, for the child
learning the language, and for the mature speaker or writer using
it to express what has not before been said, the pairing of
meanings with word-sounds is accomplished by "an unknown law" that

enables us to make use of our bodies and their natural powers of vocal gesticulation for purposes that transcend them, namely to mean, express, and understand the world as humanly comprehensible, as the intended correlate of behaviors that themselves "make sense", and confer a sense on the objects that polarize them. In this, every language is equally "natural" and equally conventional; it is natural to man to speak but no particular use of his speech apparatus, no particular "natural" language is inscribed in human nature. It is as "natural" for man to "sing the world" in Japanese as in English.

> The psycho-physiological equipment leaves a great variety of possibilities open, and there is no more here than in the realm of instinct a human nature finally and immutably given. The use a man is to make of his body is transcendent in relation to that body as a mere biological entity. It is no more natural, and no less conventional, to shout in anger or kiss in love than to call a table a "table".[30]

And the most fundamental discriminations that distinguish one language from another occur on a deeper level than that of vocabulary and syntax. One cannot learn a language by looking up the meanings of words in a lexicon, for the simple reason that one must already know the meanings of words in order to begin to use a dictionary. A child does not learn words one by one, and the adult speaker does not use words to "translate" his clear and distinct interior thought into an external representation of it.

> Here the meaning of words must be finally induced by the words themselves, or more exactly, their conceptual meaning must be formed by a kind of subtraction from a *gestural meaning*, which is immanent in speech. . . in a foreign country, I begin to understand the meaning of words through their place in a context of action, and by taking part in a communal life . . . . In fact, every language conveys its own teaching and carries its meaning into the listener's mind. A school of music or painting which is at first not understood eventually by its own action, creates its own public, if it really *says* something; that is, does so by secreting its own meaning.[31]

If Merleau-Ponty's assertions occasionally seem to go beyond the bounds of acceptable (or, at least, verifiable) theory, they nevertheless serve to bring out one central phenomenon of language

neglected in earlier theories, namely that there is a level of
phonological meaning in language "whose very existence intellectualism does not suspect".[32] He credits Saussure and phonological
analysis, not himself, for this discovery.[33]

There is a corollary to this discovery that Merleau-Ponty
orchestrates in his later works: Just as phonemes are able to
become distinctive and thus "meaningful" signs only because they
can be "opposed" according to rule to others, so all the seman-
temes and words, all units of meaningful sound in a given
language, have meaning only thanks to their possible opposition
(in the same place in a given linguistic string) to others that
could take their place. For instance a color adjective, in this
view, would take its meaning from the fact that it is opposable to
the other color adjectives of that given language and it is only
as a part of the "system" as a whole that it carries its own
distinctive meaning. Merleau-Ponty likes to cite and refer to the
following passage from Saussure above all others.

> In language there are only differences and no positive
> terms. Whether one takes the point of view of the *signifé*
> [concept] or of the *signifiant* [acoustic image] language
> contains neither ideas nor sounds which would pre-exist the
> linguistic system but only the conceptual differences and
> phonic differences which issue from the system.[34]

In short, a language as *langue*, namely as the system of (phonological) rules that are the necessary structural conditions for
speech, is not a vocabulary of signs or words but the methodical
means, the rules, a given speech community has for discriminating
one sign from another. It is at any one point in time utterly
impossible to fix the vocabulary of a given language, of a given
speaker, of a given child who is learning the language; no dictionary or lexicon is ever complete because new and incubating
changes are forever in process of becoming actual - without, however, the language *as langue*, as system, being in the least af-
fected. It is in this sense of language that we must conclude that
the child learns the language as a whole, globally, by uncon-
sciously grasping the style of its distinctive phonemic oppositions in practice, and it is in *this sense* of language that we can
and must say, for instance, that the French language preexisted
all the works of French literature and is essentially untouched by
whatever writers may use it to express.[35]

But here we come upon another paradox in Merleau-Ponty's
"structuralism". Namely, we want to ask, how is it that, if words
and linguistic signs have no meaning in and of themselves, but

only serve to mark the differences that distinguish one sign from others, how is it that words can nevertheless be understood in isolation, independently of any awareness of those forms to which they could be opposed and which could occur in the same place in a given linguistic string?[36] Even though we can grant that all the words of a language "hold one another in place"[37] and form a synchronically closed system, it is clearly not necessary (and in any case it is impossible) to know *all* the words of a given language in order to understand just any other, or to know *all* the color adjectives in a given language to understand the one I mean just now. The answer to this question, of course, takes us away from *la langue* towards *la parole* and to questions of *referential meaning* and *semantic conditions*. This question takes us away from language as the necessary, presupposed structural condition of all speaking to the *speech act* itself, and Merleau-Ponty, like all phenomenologists (and, one might add, Wittgensteinians as well), recognizes that meaning is actualized only in *use* and that the sentence (the assertion, the proposition, the question, etc.) is, in an existential and ontological sense, intentionally prior to its component parts (i.e., the morphemes and words, which can be discovered only by a later, formal analysis). Though we cannot deal with this in any detail, we are here touching on one of the most delicate points in Merleau-Ponty's interpretation of Saussure. It involves the primacy of the speech act over its formal (and logical) conditions.[38] Here it is sufficient to emphasize what, according to Merleau-Ponty, is the crowning glory of structural linguistics, namely to have discovered and enabled us to account for the phonological level of meaning in language, which is immanent to the linguistic system itself and which is independent of all questions of referentiality and semantics. This is a level of meaning, the meanings words have just through their ability to fit into just these combinations with just these other words of *this* language (which is essential to our understanding not only of the diverse possibilities for expression we find in different natural languages but also of the peculiar genius of the poetic and literary uses of language), which was completely ignored in all the earlier, primarily "intellectualistic", theories of language.

2. THE RELATION OF WORDS TO SYNTAX

Noam Chomsky has pointed out that the major defect in the linguistic structuralism of Saussure and his disciples was to believe that syntax was a relatively trivial matter. Saussure was concerned with the taxonomic analysis of strings of sounds (from left to right if written, in temporal sequence when spoken), i.e., with a "linear" analysis that neglected the various more abstract relations between the component parts of sentences which must be studied by any grammar that would go beneath the phonological surface to the logical relations of the "deep structure" not reflected in the surface string. Saussure believed that the system of language was restricted to groups of sounds and the rules of their development into words and phrases; this was, for him, *la langue*. All other considerations, including not only referentiality and semantics, *But even syntax*, lay outside the scope of linguistics proper and were to be assigned to the "accessory" realm of *la parole*, the speech act. Even if a completely fair and nuanced study of his thought would require some qualification here, this was undoubtedly the thrust of his conclusions, and it is for this reason, Chomsky argues, that there was "very little work in syntax throughout the period of structural linguistics."[39] It is also why the structural linguists, before the advent of "depth grammar" and the study of the formal rules governing grammatical transformations of various types, not only neglected but *inhibited* the "philosophical" as well as the scientific study of grammar in its own right. That was a project of the Seventeenth and Eighteenth century "philosophical grammarians" that had to be consigned to oblivion.

In this, we have to recognize Merleau-Ponty as a true disciple of Saussure. His philosophy of language gives a very small place, if any, to purely grammatical considerations. He is concerned uniquely with what we can call semiology in a narrow sense, i.e., the study of the mechanicisms of the emergence of sense within the phonological system of signs that is realized in *words*.[40] It is almost as if, for him, grammar would be found to be nothing more than a minor subdivision of phonology, and this is, no doubt, also the reason why Merleau-Ponty was so embarrassed by Husserl's proposal for an "eidetics" of language. It is only in *La prose du monde* that Merleau-Ponty takes up the Husserlian question of grammar seriously; there he discusses the "algorithmic" aspect of language, that aspect which, once we know the rule, always enables us "to go on" (as Wittgenstein would also say) and which permits the use of language for the higher purposes of scientific and theoretical thinking.[41] Thought Merleau-Ponty fully recognized that language both originates (teleologically) and culminates (existentially) in speech acts (*la parole*), which are always grammatically formed complete units of meaning, or sentences, he did not explicitly study grammatical structures for themselves. This was, he felt, the attitude toward language specifically adopted by the logician, not the linguist or the philosopher concerned concretely with the phenomenon of expression. It was the discredited approach of the "ideal langauge" experimenters and of those in search of some perfectly defined and completely explicit linguistic instrument that could, for certain ideal purposes, *take the place* of ordinary language; it was an abstact and derived approach to language that would be of little service for the illumination of productive speech. If he had been more open to syntactical considerations, he would not doubt have found that syntax is much more perfectly "translatable" from one language to another than are "words," and that the study of grammar would require the posing of a number of questions that his own theory of language avoids *in fact* if not in principle. He did recognize that *la parole* is related to *la langue* as "fact" to "essence" (in the Husserlian acceptance of these terms), not only, though perhaps primarily, in the sense that the structures of language are always *logically* already presupposed in any actual speaking, but also in the sense that the structures of *la langue* are precisely the rules *of speaking* and are, though logically presupposed in analysis, historically and ontologically generated by speech itself. The two are as inseparably united as an instance and its type.

3. THE PROBLEM OF GRAMMATICAL UNIVERSALS

To deal properly with the above-mentioned omission in Merleau-Ponty's philosophy of language, and of its possible remedies *from within his own thought* and with the resources of his own phenomenology, would require a separate and intricate treatise. Here we shall try to bring out as best we can what is at stake and show, schematically, how he could have dealt with the problem. Against the claims of "philosophical" grammarians like Husserl[42] (and, we can well believe, like Chomsky, had he known his writings), Merleau-Ponty frequently inveighs against the conception that there are certain "universal" or "eidetic" structures of language in general of which the grammar of any particular language would be only some cloudy or imperfect realization. He does not believe, at least in the central body of his writing, either that there are universal structures underlying all grammars (i.e., logically prior to any particular grammar) or that there is some *eidetic telos* of grammar towards which empirical, historical grammars can be seen to be groping.
In criticism of Husserl, he writes:

. . . we must understand that since synchrony is only a
cross-section of diachrony the system realized in it never
exists wholly in act but always involves latent or incubating
changes.

It is never composed of absolutely univocal meanings
which can be made completely explicit beneath the gaze of
transparent constituting consciousness. It will be a question
not of a system of forms of signification clearly articulated
in terms of one another – not of a structure of linguistic
ideas built according to a strict plan – but of a cohesive
whole of convergent linguistic gestures, each of which will
be defined less by a signification than by a value of usage.
Far from particular languages appearing as the "confused"
realization of certain ideal and universal forms of signification the possibility of such a synthesis becomes problema-
tical. If universality is attained, it will not be through a
universal language which would go back prior to the diversity
of languages to provide us with the foundations of all possible languages. It will be through an oblique passage from a
given language that I speak and that initiates me into the
phenomenon of expression, to another given language that I
learn to speak and that effects the act of expression according to a completely different style – the two languages
(and ultimately all given languages) being contingently comparable only at the outcome of this passage and only as
signifying wholes, without our being able to recognize in
them the common elements of one single categorial structure.[43]

Thus, though Merleau-Ponty seems, frequently and explicitly, to
rule out the possibility of linguistic universals, we must note
that he hardly ever discusses purely grammatical or syntactical
relationships as such, that he never distinguishes surface from
depth grammar (as not only Chomsky but also Wittgenstein and
Russell do), and the he always leaves the door open by qualifying
his own assertions with phrases like "if universality is attained",[44] "if there is such a thing as universal thought",[45] "but
even if these invariants exist,"[46] and similar locutions, which
seem to express doubt and qualification rather than fully convinced denial. As always, Merleau-Ponty proceeds dialectically. At
the outset we are faced, in this third paradox of language, with
two quite straightforward facts about linguistic experience. On
the one hand it seems to be well attested and theoretically well
founded to believe that all of the empirical languages known to
man are completely sufficient for all purposes of human communi-

cation, that none is privileged, that none necessarily deforms thought, that there is nothing that can be said in one language that cannot be said equally well – though, of course, using different phonological, morphological, and syntactical possibilities – in any other. This might be called the fact of the universal equivalence or translatability of each language into every other; this is particularly evident on the level of syntax but certainly extends throughout the whole domain of semantics, at least in principle.

On the other hand, there are the kinds of considerations we have seen Merleau-Ponty urging, to the effect that there are practical and theoretical limits on "translatability" and that natural languages, if only from the fact that they have diverse phonological and morphological systems, to say nothing of the diachronic developments of their syntax as well, the vicissitudes and accidental historical changes to which they are subject, etc., are not *exhaustively* translatable into one another. In his typical fashion Merleau-Ponty will not take his stand on the side of either of these opposed positions, though it is clear that he is more suspicious of the "intellectualist" than of the "empiricist" (or "skeptical" – he likes to think of himself as a "skeptic") framework. Precisely because of the fact that the ideas or concepts that language expresses can be neither entertained nor distinguished except through some particular use of language, he rejects a universality that would come "from above", so to speak, from a universal mind, a system of "innate ideas", or a power of thought that could think without the use of some language. But is this to deny *all* universality? It would seem, if we read him carefully, that he does not go this far, and we can thus pose the question more clearly. The question is not: are there some linguistic universals? but rather: what *kind* of universality do we find in language? And, if we pose the question in this way, we find that Merleau-Ponty gives, though hesitatingly, an original answer that owes a good deal both to structuralism and to phenomenology. We can briefly sketch his answer in two steps.

If there is such a thing as universal thought, it is achieved by taking up the effort towards expression and communication in *one* single language, and accepting all its ambiguities, all the suggestions and overtones of meaning of which [it] is made up, and which are the exact measure of its power of expression. . . . The meaning of a sentence appears intelligible throughout, detachable from the sentence and finitely self-subsistent in an intelligible world, because we presuppose as given all those exchanges, owed to the history of the language, which contribute to determining its sense. . . .

But in fact. . . the clearness of language stands out from an obscure background, and if we carry our research far enough we shall eventually find that language is. . . uncommunicative of anything other than itself, that its meaning is inseparable from it. We need, then, to seek the first attempts at language in the emotional gesticulation whereby man superimposes on the given world the world according to man. There is here nothing resembling the famous naturalistic conceptions which equate the artificial sign with the natural one, and try to reduce language to emotional expression. . . . It would be legitimate to speak of "natural signs" only if the anatomical organization of our body produced a correspondence between specific gestures and given "states of mind". . . . It is not enough for two conscious subjects to have the same organs and nervous system for the same emotions to produce the same signs. What is important is how they use their bodies, the simultaneous patterning of body and world in emotion. . . . Behavior creates meanings which are transcendent in relation to the anatomical apparatus, and yet immanent to the behavior as such, since it communicates itself and is understood. [47]

Here we might say that we have an existential basis for the distinction between surface grammar and depth grammar: each man makes himself understood even though each speaks his own language; were it not for social pressures and the need to conform to the institutions of the group there would be as many languages as there are people, and *in one sense* there already are. Is it not the case that in some areas such as New Guinea where tribes are numerous, small, hostile and extremely suspicious of one another, one will find two or three hundred different languages whose speakers are mutually unintelligible to one another? And, even within our own tribe, do we not each one develop our own idiolects, our own personal versions of whatever language we agree to speak for purposes of communication? We see here the ground of Merleau-Ponty's suspicion of universal structure. Perhaps the teaching of a language to an infant is not so much an effort to give him something he could not develop for himself as to prevent him from fabricating his own.

The only foundation for universality that Merleau-Ponty will accept is not the "eidetic" universality of a necessary *a priori* logical form but the comprehensibility achieved in "the oblique passage from a given language that I speak. . . to another given language that I learn."[48] The event is too hesitant and passing to imagine that some common mind or some explicit convention is responsible for it; at the same time it is too systematic, too consistent to be reducible to a series of accidents. On the one hand there is the practical impossibility of giving *one*, ideal, formal analysis of any given language that would show forth its unique rational formula, that would enable us to define its essence unequivocally and derive all its various structures from a common principle, showing their proper hierarchies and derivations. It is equally impossible to account rationally for the historical relationships between languages or to pinpoint the time, for example, at which Latin irrevocably becomes French. But, at the same time, when one takes up the linguistic history of the human race, the continuous proliferation of aberrant forms in which no structure is ever fully finished or achieved, and in which no innovation can be precisely dated, one sees that there is no precise break between any one language and any other, no clean line of demarcation between one dialect and another. At this point, says Merleau-Ponty, one sees that "to be precise, *there is only one language in a state of becoming.*"[49]

> If we must renounce the abstract universality of a rational grammar which would give us the common essence of all languages, we rediscover at the same time the concrete universality of a given language which is becoming different from itself while remaining the same. Because I am now speaking, my language is not for me a sum of facts but a unified instrument for a complete intention of expression. And *because it is so for me I am able to enter into other systems of expression,* at first by grasping them as variants of my own, and then by letting myself be inhabited by it until my own language becomes a variant of it. Neither the unity of language, nor the distinctions among languages, nor their historical derivations from one another cease to be understandable just because we refuse to conceive one essence of language. It is simply that they must be conceived not from the standpoint of the concept or of essence but from the dimension of existence.[50]

There is, therefore, an experienced and "existential" foundation for universality in language, but it is not that of the "innate ideas" of the Cartesians or of the logical *a prioris* of "rational grammar". It is rather the "oblique" or "lateral" universality of incomplete but sufficient comprehensibility that we effect in actually speaking to others. We must each speak according to

common rules or we would not be understood, and yet each act of
speech is, in each case, a "coherent deformation" of the rules
already given and accepted. In his essay on Levi-Strauss Merleau-
Ponty applies the same conception to social structures.

> There thus appears at the base of social systems a
> formal infrastructure (one is tempted to say an unconscious
> thought), an anticipation of the human mind, as if our scien-
> ce were already completed in events, and the human order of
> culture a second order of nature dominated by other in-
> variants. But even if these invariants exist, even if social
> science were to find beneath structures a metastructure to
> which they conformed (as phonology does beneath phonemes),
> the universal we would thus arrive at could no more be sub-
> stituted for the particular than general geometry annuls the
> local truth of Euclidean spatial relations. . . . The impli-
> cations of a formal structure may well bring out the internal
> necessity of a given genetic sequence. *But it is not these
> implications which make men, society, and history
> exist. . . . This process of joining objective analysis to
> lived experience is perhaps the most proper task of anthro-
> pology. . . . This provides a second way to the universal: no
> longer the overarching universal of a strictly objective
> method, but a sort of lateral universal* which we acquire
> through ethnological experience and its incessant testing of
> the self through the other person and the other person
> through the self.[51]

We are thus brought, in our schematic analysis of Merleau-Ponty's
thought on this subject, to the final step in his argument. It is
one that preoccupied him throughout his writings and that ties his
own phenomenological method to Husserl's, namely his attempt to
understand the relationship between "fact" and "essence", the
instance and the type, induction and eidetic intuition (*Wesenschau*). In this same essay on Levi-Strauss he refers to "the old
prejudice which opposes deduction to induction." He had examined
this in some detail in his essay on "Phenomenology and the Sciences of Man", and he returned to it especially in the methodological sections of *The Visible and the Invisible*.

To be brief, Merleau-Ponty argues that not only in the human,
but in *all* the sciences "pure inductivity is a myth", that there
is no fruitful research that is "a pure inventorying of constants
in themselves."[52] Actual thinking moves back and forth between
experiencing and intellectual construction.[53] When one brings a
particular instance under a general law, one "reads its essence"

by adopting an "idealizing fiction" that is founded on the facts, and in terms of which the facts make sense. Such a structure or "essence", thanks to the comprehensive and interpretive imagination of the scientific investigator, is not a natural or cultural force in its own right, but a "light" that enables us to clarify concrete experience. It is no insight into an essence if one cannot turn to the corresponding individuals, the set of instances of which it is the "essence", and we know that Husserl himself "never obtained one sole *Wesenschau* that he did not subsequently take up again and rework, not to disown it, but in order to make it say what at first it had not quite said."[54] This is because there can be no knowledge of facts that does not involve some insight into their "invariant" structures, but at the same time these "invariant" structures are nothing at all but the structures the facts themselves exhibit as they are situated and organized from the point of view of the reflective scientist. One never just collects facts, and even when one has collected a large number for some purpose, one selects from among them a finite number through a "free variation" in imagination in order to construct the "idea" that will render them comprehensible: "that which cannot be varied without the object itself disappearing is the essence."[55]

> . . . philosophy does not possess the truth about language and the world from the start, but is rather the recuperation and first formulation of a Logos scattered out in our world and our life and bound to their concrete structures. . . the contrast between fact and essence [is] explicitly mediated by the idea that the purest reflection discloses a "genesis of meaning" [*Sinngenesis*] immanent in its objects – the need for each manifestation of its objects to have a "before" and an "after" and to develop through a series of steps or stages in which each step anticipates and is taken up in a subsequent one. . . . Of course this intentional history is not simply the sum of all manifestations taken one by one. *It takes them up again and puts them in order*; in the actuality of a present it reanimates and rectifies a genesis which could miscarry without it. But it can do so only in contact with what is given, *by seeking its motives within it.* It is not just an unfortunate accident that the study of significations and the study of facts encroach upon one another. If it did not condense a certain development of *truth*, a signification would be empty. . . . Superficially considered, our inherence [in history] destroys all truth; considered radically, it founds a new idea of truth. As long as I cling to the ideal of an absolute spectator, or

knowledge with no point of view, I can see my situation as nothing but a source of error. But if I have once recognized that through it I am grafted onto every action and all knowledge which can have a meaning for me, and that step by step it contains everything which can *exist* for me, then my contact with the social in the finitude of my situation is revealed to me as the point of origin of all truth, including scientific truth. And since we have an idea of truth, since we are in truth and cannot escape it, the only thing left for me to do is to define a truth in the situation. . . . Ultimately, our situation is what links us to the whole of human experience. . . . *"science". . . designates the effort to construct ideal variables which objectify and schematize the functions of this effective communication.*[56]

Husserl and Merleau-Ponty developed a phenomenological method that was neither deductive nor purely empirical.[57] Merleau-Ponty became while writing "Phenomenology and the Sciences of Man", interested in structural linguistics primarily, I think, because it presented him with the best example, and the *only* example at that time, of a science that could formulate "essential" or structural laws that still clearly participated in the historicity, contingency, and open-endedness of the primary data they themselves thematized. It showed how essential laws, which ordinarily lie beneath the threshold of experience, can nevertheless be shown to be the necessary structural conditions of the experience of which they are the laws. It gave him one of the clearest illustrations of the correlativity of fact and essence in experience and thus the means of bringing structuralism and phenomenology together and of reconciling them in a higher synthesis. All the phonological, morphological, syntactic, and other laws that govern the speech act and make it possible can clearly be shown to be *necessary* (and "invariant") laws, i.e., insofar as they thematize conditions without which speaking would be impossible, and yet these laws are themselves generated by historical, contingent acts of speech, which they serve and which they are *of.* They have no "substantiality" in themselves. (In the words of Saussure, "language is not a substance but a form".) The ultimate unity of *la langue* and *la parole*, that is, of the structural conditions and of their actualizations in the experiences that confer on them their ontological validity, is what Merleau-Ponty was striving to understand and account for on the structuralist basis provided by Saussure. This is the primary source and inspiration of everything he wrote on the philosophy of language in his middle and later periods.

CHAPTER II

THE
SIGNIFICANCE OF MERLEAU-PONTY'S
PHILOSOPHY OF LANGUAGE

1. STATEMENT OF THE PROBLEM

It is now quite a few years since we first heard of the untimely death of Maurice Merleau-Ponty. To me, and I am sure to many others, it seems much longer. Merleau-Ponty has already entered the history of philosophy. Nearly all of his writings have by now appeared in English translation, but philosophers of our generation had already enshrined his major work, the *Phenomenology of Perception*, as a "classic" even before his death. But unlike many other "classical" philosophers, Merleau-Ponty's work impresses us by its unfinished, open-ended, still-to-be-completed character. Unlike a Spinoza or an Aquinas, or even a Husserl ("the perpetual beginner"), he left his major philosophical task essentially incomplete at the time of his death. Though we cannot conceive of the phenomenological movement without his name and contribution, it is hard to think of Merleau-Ponty's thought as susceptible of generating "disciples." He achieved no system. Spinoza has disciplines; Aquinas has disciples; Hume has disciples; Husserl has disciples, and even the Logical Positivists had disciples - Merleau-Ponty can only have continuators, that is, persons who have somehow managed to grasp the difficult inner movement of his thought and who are thereby compelled to take up the problems with which he was wrestling and thus to continue to develop them. The purpose of these few brief remarks[1] will be to outline the structure of what I take to be his primary, unresolved problem and to assess its significance in a preliminary way for us contemporary philosophers.

That the thought of a philosopher who was happy to call himself not only a "phenomenologist" but, *at the same time*, a "Marxist," and an "existentialist," and who gloried in his title as "the philosopher of ambiguity," should present us with an unfinished and open-ended corpus hardly surprises us. Moreover, it is possible to detect, particularly in his later writings, signs of frustration over his not being able to make more rapid progress in working out the program which he had explicitly formulated as early as 1946[2] as the major philosophical goal of his life's

work. This goal was certainly *not unambitious*; it was to take its
point of departure in a phenomenology of perception, thence to go
on to an investigation of the higher-order levels of conscious
experience founded on perception, finally to culminate in the
formulation of a transcendental metaphysics "which would at the
same time give us the principle of an ethics."[3]

When Merleau-Ponty presented himself as a candidate for a
chair of philosophy to the body of professors of the Collège de
France in February 1952, he furnished them with a comprehensive
plan for future research which would, by building on the works he
had already published in the fields of the phenomenology of perception, art, and history, proceed to the investigation of the
realms of speaking and writing (in a projected work to be called
La prose du monde), of thinking and knowing (in a book to be
called *L'Origine de la verite*) and which would, after having thus
established a theory of truth, culminate in a metaphysical treatise, *L'Homme transcendental.* As we know, none of these works was
completed during his lifetime. He abandoned *La Prose du monde*
(less than half completed) that same year, 1952, and seems to have
definitively lost interest in it after 1959.[4] The manuscripts that
had been entitled variously "L'Origine de la verite," "Genealogie
du vrai," and "Etre et monde," were all put together after 1959
under the new title, *The Visible and the Invisible*, the book that
Merleau-Ponty was working on at the time of his death, which we
possess in the posthumous form of a half-completed treatise
followed by an intriguing but unfinished mass of "working notes."
As for *L'Homme transcendental*, the ultimate metaphysical conclusion towards which he was working, there is hardly a trace except
for what we can now work out for ourselves along the lines he had
projected, by discovering in the texts he has left us the true
intentional thread of his unfinished thought.

From 1946 onwards, once the *Phenomenology of Perception* had
been completed, Merleau-Ponty began to speak of the "immense
task"[5] which lay before him of investigating the relationships
which obtain "between intellectual consciousness and perceptual
consciousness"[6] and of establishing thereby the differences,
similarities and interrelations which obtain between "ideal truth
and perceived truth."[7] In the *Phenomenology of Perception* he had
already tried to show how the least perception possesses an "ideal
of truth," which it cannot at each moment fully account for but
which is nevertheless "the horizon of its operations."[8]

When I stand before a landscape in the company of a friend,
and attempt to point out to him the bird sitting on the limb of
the tree some fifty yards ahead of us, or the face of the owl in
one of the clouds passing overhead, I make a demand on him with

this perceptual situation that is a claim for the objectively necessary and universally valid truth of my own perceptions. There is not in this experience *my private world* juxtaposed to *his private world* which we can communicate to one another only by using linguistic signs that enable us to analogize each other's experiences; rather, there is given but one "objective" world – in the phenomenological sense of "objective" – correlative to our acts of perception and to any other possible acts of perception into which we are both "geared." If my friend does not yet see what I see, I insistently point it out even to the point of becoming impatient; I *demand* that what I see be seen by him also. This is because in the smallest perception there is given – as the very meaning of that perception – the claim that what I see here before me now must be seen by any other perceiver who would stand where I am standing. That my present perception may require later revision and reinterpretation is totally irrelevant to *this* experience of the ideally objective truth of *this* perception. Whatever corrections later experience may bring to what is now an immediate, present experience, my present perceptual experience here and now of just these objects just now before me requires that I recognize them as being objectively "true,," i.e., that they are really there just as I perceive them.[9] And this is an eidetic, not merely an empirical, claim about perception.

The same, according to Merleau-Ponty, is the case for the experiences of freedom, choice and value. Like all other experiences, evaluative experiences take place in temporal sequences which are undergirded by the perceptual awareness of my being in a "place" (i.e., my body) through time. *Since* every perceptual experience, in turn, is a "pro-ject" (i.e., a leap towards the not-yet-experienced future) within a field of possibilities, and *since* whatever aspect of a thing I may be presently given is surrounded and escorted by an infinite field of other possible presentations and other possible explorations of this same thing, *to say* that this thing is now presented to me from this given angle is to imply that there is no intrinsic necessity for its being so presented, that it *could* be presented otherwise, and that in fact I experience *whatever* perceptual objects may be given to me as being experienced and as being experienceable from an indefinite number of other perspectives – perspectives which I do not now occupy *de facto*, but which I *could*, at least in principle, occupy *de jure*. Thus there is a subjunctivity to perceptual experience which is the experienced perceptual foundation of freedom. Since no particular approach to reality is fatally inscribed either in nature or in history, there is a margin of indeterminacy for human free choice which is the foundation of "objective" value.[10]

According to Merleau-Ponty, therefore, perception as the most basic stratum of experience "is our presence at the moment when things, truths, values are constituted for us; . . . perception is a nascent *logos*; . . . it teaches us, outside all dogmatism, the true conditions of objectivity . . . it summons us to the tasks of knowledge and action."[11] There is here no question "of reducing human knowledge to sensation," but rather of recovering "the consciousness of rationality" that lives in perceptual conscious-ness and that founds the unity that we experience between all the diverse levels of intentionality. Merleau-Ponty does not attempt to reduce the higher-order structures of thought and value to perception but rather to show how the most fundamental structures of perception reappear in a transformed and more complex, but still recognizable, manner in such higher-order activities as speaking, thinking, reasoning, imagining, choosing, evaluating, knowing, etc. Thus we see that the phenomenology of perception leads to the posing of the question of the relationships which obtain between perceiving consciousness and all the other levels of consciousness that are "founded" on it.

For traditional philosophers Merleau-Ponty's *Phenomenology of Perception* appeared to be, on first reading, a rather strange document. In what other, historical account of perception was it ever found necessary to include discussions of sexuality, affec-tivity, thought (*cogito*), freedom, temporality, and even of mathe-matical and formal reasoning? Are *these*, also, *perception*? Clear-ly, the phenomenology of perception, in Merleau-Ponty's eyes, involves the whole of philosophy and leads us into a new way of posing the most fundamental questions.

In this paper we are concerned only with the central thread, namely the investigation of the relationship between thought (language-using consciousness) and perception (the prelinguistic objectification of the world). This is the study of the nexus of these various structures of experience which Husserl terms *Fun-dierung.* For Merleau-Ponty this problem took the form of a special investigation of the relation of apriori truth to factual or empirical truth, and it led him to attempt to show that they were somehow mutually implicating, only two facets of the same ex-perience, apparently situated within a continuum of experience, rather than being absolutely and apodictically opposed as two different ways of knowing.

Thus *every factual truth is a rational truth, and vice versa.* The   relation of reason to fact, or eternity to time, like that of reflec tion to the unreflective, of thought to language or of thought to perception is this two-way relationship that phenomenology has called *Fundierung*: the founding term, or originator – time, the unreflective, the fact, language, perception – is primary in the sense that *the originated* is presented as a determinate or explicit form of *the originator*, which prevents the latter from reabsorbing the former, and yet *the originator* is not primary in the empiricist sense and *the originated* is not *simply derived*, since it is *through the originated that the originator is made manifest.* [12]

2. THE RELATION OF LANGUAGE TO PERCEPTION

This seems to me to be one of the most pregnant and important statements of his fundamental problem that Merleau-Ponty has left us. It is a thesis that stands at the center of his work; it is not something that either he or Husserl claimed to have demonstrated; it is rather the framework of their phenomenological investigations, a working hypothesis that would have to be worked out by a generation of phenomenologists. And it seems – let us admit it at once – to present us with almost insuperable problems. On the one hand there is the "objectivity" characteristic of perceived objects in the real world; on the other hand there is the "objectivity" characteristic of such ideal (linguistic) entities as analytic and synthetic a priori truths and their *logical* implications. In his memoir to the College de France of 1952 Merleau-Ponty wrote:

> I found in the experience of the perceived world a new type of relation between the mind and truth. The evidence of the perceived thing lies in its concrete aspect, in the very texture of its quali ties, and in the equivalence among all its sensible properties – which caused Cezanne to say that one should be able to paint even odors. Before our undivided existence the world is true; it exists. The unity, the articulations of both are intermingled. We experience in it a truth which shows through and envelops us rather than being held and circumscribed by our mind. [13]

Hence the proper philosophical approach to the problems of perception is not to ask, from the standpoint of a dogmatically rationalistic theory of truth, whether we *really* perceive the world, but rather to begin with the phenomenological decision to call *what we in fact perceive* "the world." As he says in another place:

"The [perceived] thing imposes itself not as true for every intel-
lect, but as real for every subject who is standing where I am."[14]
   But it is characteristic of perceptual truth and of perceptual reality to be always incomplete, subject to revision, never
adequately given, intrinsically in need of reinterpretation in the
future, and thus subject to a process of unending and never com-
pleteable verification. Any empirical fact in or about the world
can never have more than a "presumptive" validity.
   This does not seem to be the case, however, for "the field of
knowledge properly so called - i.e., the field in which the mind
seeks to possess the truth, to define its objects itself, and thus
to attain to a universal wisdom, not tied to the particularities
of our situation."[15]
   Merleau-Ponty thus recognizes the sharp distinction between
"factual truth" and "rational truth." It is characteristic of
apriori truths to be true independent of any appeal to experience.
Since they are based on language rather than on *that to which*
language enables us to refer (i.e., the real world), they are
matters of meaning only and are thus ideally independent of the
world of *real* facts and events.
   We are, therefore, confronted with an *aporia* and we are
perplexed. Merleau-Ponty delighted in such perplexities (*aporiai*).
At the same time, we are - from the beginning - in no doubt about
what Merleau-Ponty's *conclusion* is going to be. But we are sometimes uncertain about how he is going to reach it, as he undoubtedly was also - since he was unable to finish his book on *The
Origin of Truth.* He adopts, he tells us, a "methodological rationalism" (as opposed to the "dogmatic rationalism" of a
Hegel),[16] by which he means a conceptual, and therefore eidetic,
investigation of the meaning of various kinds of experience. But
how does the *eidos* emerge in experience?
   In his phenomenology of perception he showed that we are
given a single, objectively unified "world," conditionally "true"
for any possible experiencer (this "lived world" being the only
field within which human choice and action can take place). Later,
in his historical writings he developed the notion of

       the idea of a single history or of a logic of history
   [which is]   implied in the least human exchange, in the
   least social perception.   For example, anthropology supposes
   that civilizations very different   from ours are comprehensible to us, that they can be situated in   relation to ours
   and vice-versa, that all civilizations belong to the   same
   universe of thought, *since the least use of language implies
   an   idea of truth.* Also we can never pretend to dismiss the

adventures of   history as something foreign to our present
action, since even the   most independent search for the most
abstract truth has been and is a   factor of history. . . .
All human acts and all human creations con stitute a single
drama, and in this sense we are all saved or lost   together.
Our life is essentially universal.[17]

Finally, though he feared and denigrated Husserl's attempt to
establish the basis for a universal, apriori, formal grammar,
nevertheless in his writings on the philosophy of language and
particularly in his unfinished and unpublished *La prose du monde*
he developed his own explanation of the universality of meaning
and intention which is postulated in *the very attempt* of one man
to address another. There are not, he concludes in this manuscript, *many* languages: "to be precise," he writes, "there is only
one language in a state of becoming."[18]

But our problem is not to discover from his texts what
Merleau-Ponty saw either as the point of departure or as the
ultimate goal of his own thought; this is perfectly clear. *Our
problem is with what stands in between* As was intimated above in
Chapter I when discussing Merleau-Ponty's method, it is clear that
he always proceeds dialectically, using an existentialist version
of what analytical philosophers call "Ramsey's Maxim." Ramsey's
Maxim states that in those cases in which apparently antithetical
or contradictory positions - neither of which is satisfactory
- are in conflict, "it is a heuristic maxim that the truth lies
not in one of the two disputed views but in some third possibility
which has not yet been thought of, which we can only discover by
rejecting something assumed as obvious by both of the dis-
putants."[19]

Merleau-Ponty's method is to reconcile two opposed positions
in a higher synthesis which will explain why each of the alterna-
tives is indisputably right from its own perspective but yet makes
an error (in the form of some fatal assumption) - which is, for
the sake of the elegance of the presentation, found to be the *same*
on both sides - and then to show that, once this error is elimi-
nated, both of the supposedly competing explanations can be incorporated in a new and more comprehensive explanation which now
accounts for both without conceding the right completely to
either. Thus in discussing the relations between necessary, universally valid, and therefore apriori ("conceptual") truths on the
one hand and perceptual truth on the other, Merleau-Ponty denies
the rights of neither side; he accepts all the evidence which the
rationalists and empiricists have accumulated, and yet attempts to
show that these are not necessarily two opposed, absolutely

different, completely isolable ways of knowing, but that one is "founded" on the other. Perceptual consciousness, which operates according to the dumb rules of objectivity which govern the constitution of perceptual objects (and which are revealed in a phenomenology of perception) gives us the *real world* of things and events, and *this* world of perception is the "founding term" or, he says, the "originator" of thought. The structures of thought are therefore of a different order from the structures of perception – which are "absolutely" prior to thought – but at the same time it is only through thought that the structures of perception are "made manifest."

We need not dwell over a few already well-understood points. Clearly the sense of "origin" or "priority" hear is not temporal or historical, but logical; the same consciousness which *perceives* the world also *thinks* it, and language (or thought) is contemporaneous with the silent objectifications that surround it and that it enables us to articulate. Secondly, we need not dwell on Merleau-Ponty's obvious delight in showing that categorial, conceptual thinking takes time, that every new theory and every new idea originates in determinate cultural surroundings as the answer to some determinate question, that each idea carries its "date" and has its "birthplace,"[20] since this would be admitted by empiricists and intellectualists alike and in no way affects the logical independence of *what is thought* from its psychological and historical conditions.

What is more important is to see the way in which an apriori truth can be fitted into new historical contexts and thus have its significance altered, not only with reference to the really perceived world but also with reference to other categorial schemes that it itself "founds" or makes possible. "Once launched, and committed to a certain set of thoughts, Euclidean space, for example, or the conditions governing the existence of a certain society, I discover evident truths; but these are not unchallengeable, since perhaps this space or this society are not the only ones possible. It is therefore of the essence of certainty to be established only with reservations. . . ."[21]

Merleau-Ponty orchestrates his mediating viewpoint with examples taken from geometry. This is particularly pertinent inasmuch as geometrical truths figure most prominently among those which such arch-rationalists as Husserl unequivocally situated in "the kingdom of truth," as not being in any way dependent on empirical experience or science, as being strictly apriori, known deductively from self-evident axioms, independent of time and of any and all "psychologism."

Merleau-Ponty takes as his primary example our perceptual intuition of the eidos "triangle." His argument here is based on an analysis of our actual, intuitive "perception" of the eidos "triangle" which precedes and "founds" all the later and derived deductions and proofs which we may formulate linguistically about this eidos. For instance, if I want to *prove* that the angles of a triangle are equal to two right angles, such a truth is not evident from the inspection of the figure of the triangle and is not known simply from the fact that, having grasped the eidos "triangle" I am able to repeat the operation of recognizing triangles – as closed, three-sided, rectilinear figures – in an indefinite number of empirical figures. From my perceptual grasp of this eidos I can proceed to a conceptual (i.e., verbal) explication of what this essence implies for objective thought, such as, for instance, proving that the sum of its angles equals two right angles.

The necessity of the proof is not an analytic necessity: the con struction which enables the conclusion (namely, that the angles of a triangle are equal to two right angles) to be reached is not really contained in the essence of the triangle, but merely possible when that essence serves as a starting point. There is no definition of a triangle [such as a "closed, three-sided, rectilinear figure"] which includes in advance the properties subsequently to be demonstrated and the intermediate steps leading to that demonstration. Extending one side, drawing through the apex a line parallel to the opposite side, introducing the theorem relating to parallels and their secant, these steps are possible only if I consider the triangle itself as it is drawn on the paper, on the blackboard or in the imagination, with its physiognomy, the concrete arrangement of its lines, in short its *Gestalt*. [22]

In short, the formalization of this proof is always a "retrospective" drawing out of the relationships which are already given dumbly in perceptual intuition. "Formal thought feeds on intuitive thought," he says, and in reality true certainty arises from intuitive experience, "even though, or rather *precisely because*, the principles [made explicit by formal thought] are tacitly assumed there." Without the primordial intuition "there would be no experience of truth," nor would there by any possibility of thinking formally "*vi formae*. . . if formal relations were not first presented to us crystalized in some particular thing." The ability to think out the categorial implications of the truth

already given in perceptual experience issues in linguistic statements which mutually implicate each other and thus have the demon-
strative value of deduced truths "because I cause [this demonstra-
tion] to emerge from the dynamic formula of the triangle. It
expresses "my power" *to think* no less than *to perceive* "the triangle's structure."

> I "consider" the triangle, which is for me a set of
> lines with a   certain orientation, and if words such as
> "angle" or "direction" have   any meaning for me, it is in so
> far as I place myself at a point, and   from it tend towards
> another point, in so far as the system of   spatial positions
> provides me with a field of possible movements. . . . In so
> far as the triangle [is] implied in my hold on the world, it
> [is] bursting with indefinite possibilities of which the
> construction actually drawn was merely one. . . . Far from
> its being the case that geometrical thinking transcends per-
> ceptual consciousness, it is from the world of perception
> that I borrow the notion of essence. *I believe* that the
> triangle *has always had*, and *always will have*, angles the sum
> of which equals two right angles, as well as all the other
> less obvious properties which geometry attributes to it,
> because I have had the experience of a real triangle, and
> because, as a physical thing, it necessarily *has* within
> itself everything that it has ever been able, or ever will be
> able, to display. Unless the thing perceived had forever im-
> planted within us the ideal notion of being which is what it
> is, there would be no phenomenon of being. . . . What I call
> the essence of the triangle is nothing but this presumption
> of a completed synthesis, in terms of which we have defined
> the thing.[23]

These reflections enable us to see how certain supposedly
atemporal truths and relationships can later be fitted into new
contexts and new horizons of thought and explanation in which they
will take on new significance, and it also shows that even in a
purely eidetic science like geometry the content of this science,
at any one particular historical period, differs from that of
others, in the function of the questions which are asked, and in
the particular possibilities which are chosen among those present
within the whole field of "infinite possibilities" implied in
originary experience.

3. THE DIALECTICAL SOLUTION

Nevertheless, we can still ask whether this is a completely satisfactory account of the relations of thought to perception, and
especially whether it is fully capable of giving a satisfactory
meaning to the surprising statement with which we began, namely
that "every factual truth is a rational truth, and *vice versa.*"[24]
Has Merleau-Ponty clearly shown - or only asserted - that the
"real triangle. . . as a physical thing. . . *necessarily has*
within itself" all its ideal mathematical properties? He says that
the "essence [eidos] of the triangle" is nothing other than the
ideal presumption of the kind of "completed synthesis in terms of
which we have defined the thing." But there is this difficulty:
the perceptual synthesis of the various possible presentations of
a physical thing can never, in principle, be completed, whereas
the eidetic intuition of the mathematical properties of such
things as triangles can be *adequately* (as well as apodictically)
established on the basis of the most inadequately given example,
and without ever returning to the "real" example again at all. Is
there only a difference of degree here?

The difficulty is that certain truths, among them geometrical
and other logical and mathematical truths (to leave out of account
altogether the synthetic and material aprioris lurking in the
background) are *formally* true, and can thus be known to be true in
virtue of their conceptual content alone and without referring
them back to experience. What we *mean* by a rational truth is that
it cannot possibly be false and that its truth can be established
independently of future experience. Rational truths can be fitted
into new contexts; they can be more fully developed and more fully
comprehended at some future time than they are now, but it will
never turn out that they were simply false. *On the contrary,*
factual truths about "real" and "physical" things are given in
perceptual presentations which must be forever incomplete and
subject to future correction. Any factual truth can turn out to be
false; its only "necessity" is first that it will always remain
true that it *appeared* to me, or to my culture, or to my historical
epoch, to have been true at some time, and it may be that it is
thanks to my (or our) *temporary* acceptance of its truth that we
are now able to reach a new synthesis in which it is still incorporated but within the context of which it is now seen to have
been "false." *This* is the only kind of "necessity" perceptual
truth can have, namely, as provisional, revisible, at any time no
more than *presumptively* "necessary," "universal," or "true."[25]
This is not what we understand by conceptual or apriori truth.

The mere fact that "linguistic truth,"[26] if we can call it that, originates from experience and *can* refer back to experience does not seem to be sufficient to *account for* the radical distinction between meaning and referentiality which language introduces into experience, and therefore into the articulation of the experienced world. The problems of the interrelations of speech and perception are not *all* solved simply by showing that language-using-consciousness is a logically posterior explicitation of what perception has already accomplished, because, even if this be the case, it may be that we have the articulated world of perception that we have precisely because of the potentialities that the linguistic expression of meaning introduces into experience. Merleau-Ponty clearly began to wonder whether this might not be the case in the last pages of his chapter on "The *Cogito*" in the *Phenomenology of Perception*, and this unsettling premonition seems to have been the vital impetus behind his more and more exclusive turn to the study of language. His impatience at not being able to find the key to his perplexities must account for his abandoning *La prose du monde*, as well as for his final attempt after 1959 to change his mind about publishing *L'Origine de la verite*. We will not, of course, attempt to accomplish here what he himself was incapable of, but only to isolate the central thread of his thought on these problems and to *suggest* an explanation for his inability to accomplish his task.

From the simple historical fact that from the years 1949–1950 onwards Merleau-Ponty's writings on language begin to multiply greatly in number, we may wonder whether he was ever satisfied with the manner in which he had claimed to resolve the relations between "factual truth" and "rational truth" in the *Phenomenology of Perception*. But even more pertinent evidence of his dissatisfaction with his early solution of this problem is provided by the observation that his philosophy of language grows considerably more complex, that it introduces a radical reinterpretation of the "gestural" theory of language espoused in his early writings, and that it takes up not only the central focal point of all his later philosophical thought, but that it also takes on the role of becoming *the essential paradigm* in terms of which we are finally asked, in *The Visible and the Invisible*, to understand even perceptual consciousness itself.

Time does not permit me to repeat, or even to summarize, what I have already argued elsewhere on this point, but it is important to note that in his inaugural lecture at the Collège de France in 1953, and consistently thereafter, particularly in *La Prose du monde*, he credits Saussure (and linguistic structuralism generally) with providing us with a "theory of signs" that is not only a

better basis for a philosophy of history than anything we find in
Hegel or Marx, but also for a "new conception of reason" in its
relation to the other modalities of experience.[27]
    In the *Phenomenology of Perception* his chapter on "The Body
as Expression and Speech," though an important part of the whole
project, discusses the phenomenon of linguistic expression as but
one aspect (integral but at the same time peripheral) of the
perceptual objectification of objects. He sees – a thesis he never
retracted nor ever needed to retract – that *words* have a
"gestural" function and are, indeed, *like* gestures in that they
express a meaning which is not objectifiable or expressible
without their physical "incarnation" in bodily acts. Meanings are
not "attached to" words, any more than they are to gestures;
rather words and gestures are the very lived conditions of the
possibility of the expression of meaning at all. For this reason
(which is full of very important implications) the study of
language has a place, though a limited and subordinate one, within
the architectonic of the *Phenome-nology of Perception* as a whole.
It also has a place because of the preconceptual, "affective,"
"existential," level of meaning which phonemics introduces into
the objectification of things by enabling us to grasp and express
their "emotional essence" prior to conceptualization – in the very
melody and intonations of the phonemic modulations of a particular
language.
    In his later writings, primarily under the influence of
Saussure and structural linguistics, he greatly extends the role
of language in his theoretical explanation of the various objectifications which constitute the world of objects among which we
live.
    The first step in this development was to elaborate a theory
of the relationship of language and speech to "silence." This he
accomplished in the writings which date from the period of his
assuming his new chair at the Collège de France.[28] We cannot
pursue this in complete detail here, but it is possible to get
some idea of what Merleau-Ponty means by the "silence" which
surrounds language and enables it *to occur as speech* if we recognize the distinction between *la langue* and *la parole*, which he
was elaborating at this time. On the one hand speech-acts, exer-
cises of *la parole*, institute *la langue* and make it live, but on
the other hand speech itself is possible only on the background of
all the subunderstood phonological, morphological, and syntactical
rules, as well as within the context of the particular lexicon, of
our *langue*. We use *la langue* in the way we use our bodies, without
thought and without explicit consciousness of the structures which
we are bringing into action at any one point. The first meaning of

the "silence" which makes speech possible is that of *la langue*, which does not itself speak but which is the *ground* of all speech. This "silence" is not unstructured, it is highly determinate. Moreover – and this is even more important – our social acts of speaking, the speech-acts of *la parole* (our particular usages of our common language in each particular case), result in a kind of "coherent deformation" of the already sedimented meanings and intentions which form the silent background for our speech and which is constituted of all the forms, all the linguistic institutions of the historical tradition of our distinctive linguistic culture. We speak, in short, with a complex, determinate and already articulated matrix of linguistic structures as a background, which at each instant enables our speech-acts to take place, and thus enables us to break the silence and to say something new in authentic and original acts of meaning. Thus *la parole* brings about a constant dislocation and continuing change in *la langue*. We may use the same words as we have used on previous occasions, or the same words as the great thinkers and philosophers, the classical writers of our literary tradition have used, but the meaning of these words is never fully grasped and transmitted once and for all; the very meaning of our words is itself a limit-concept which eludes speech by always escaping beyond it into the transcendental silence of the realm of conceptual thought, which, while polarizing our attempts at expression, always escapes us to some extent, and thus always leaves room for more to be said, for our *langue* to be used by countless other speakers and writers for *their* purposes and for *their* intentions. And *their* purposes and intentions will, in turn, introduce us into *new* realms of linguistic meaning which are nevertheless comprehensible and communicable to all on the basis of a common understanding and acceptance of the structures of *this* language, an acceptance of common rules which is *sufficient* for all purposes of communication, but which is never fully *adequate* to bring expression to completion.

But unfortunately, Merleau-Ponty neither finished nor ever published the final systematic development of these theses about language in *La Prose du monde*. Thus in his middle period he did not ever achieve the unification of his incipient thoughts on the philosophy of language – which we find in the plethora of essays he wrote during those years on various isolated aspects of linguistic meaning and expression, and on the philosophy of language in general – in any finished theoretical form.

Finally, we must observe that from 1959 onwards he attempted to incorporate his incipient reflections on a theory of "Speech and Silence" into the much broader framework of *The Visible and the Invisible.* The background silence of *la langue* and the context of discourse which enables authentic acts of new speaking to take place, is but *one* of the structures of what, in his final work, he called "the invisible." The ultimate significance of his thought, particularly as a philosopher of language concerned with the relationship of language to perception and to truth, lies in working out the theory of speech and perception that he sketched in this final, posthumously published volume.

Again, we can do no more here than delineate the general problematic and relate the theory presented in *The Visible and the Invisible* to his central problem of the relationship between thought (or language) on the one hand to perception on the other. Let me sketch out very briefly the final proposal he made on this matter in the closing pages of *The Visible and the Invisible*.[29] Merleau-Ponty here attempts to show that the human body, as a system of structured possibilities for future action, which are realized in the "objectification" and in the very "discovery" of perceptual objects, is "structured like language." Language, as he saw it, following Saussure is a "diacritical, relative, opposi- tional system" of elements which are not "absolute" bits of meaning but rather only "divergencies" (*écarts*) sufficient to enable us to establish a system of linguistic signs or *words* (in which all the phonological, morphological and syntactical struc- tures of our language terminate, because, after all, language is constituted only of *words*), which themselves have meaning for us only because they are opposable, according to rule, to all the other linguistic signs or *words*, of the same category and level, that our language permits. It is the task of the philosopher of language, ultimately, to show how linguistic structures mirror and analogize the structures of perception and thus enable us to understand the structures of action which give us our primordial motives for distinguishing one object, or any aspect of an object, from any other, and how they thus produce, emanating from the active subject (as an embodied consciousness), the actual lived world of our perceptual experience.

Just as we say that it is a part of the meaning of a color adjective in the English language (such as, for instance, "red" or "brown") that *any other* color adjective in the lexicon of that language *could* (from the point of view of purely formal syntacti- cal analysis) take its place, according to rule, in a given lin- guistic string, so Merleau-Ponty wants to say that colors them- selves, as perceived, are not so much "things" as "a difference between things." Let me refer briefly to his analysis of the perception of the color "red":

A punctuation in the field of red things, which includes the tiles of roof tops, the flags of gatekeepers and of the Revolution, certain terrains near Aix or Madagascar, it is also a punctuation in the field of red garments, which includes, along with the dresses of women, robes of professors, bishops, and advocate generals, and also in the field of adornments and that of uniforms. And its red literal ly is not the same as it appears in one constellation or in the other, as the pure essence of the Revolution of 1917 precipitates in it, or that of the eternal feminine, or that of the public prosecu tor, or that of the gypsies dressed like hussars who reigned twenty- five years ago over an inn on the Champs-Elysees. A certain red is also a fossil drawn up from the depths of imaginary worlds. If we took all these participations into account, we would recognize that a naked color, and in general a visible, is not a chunk of absolutely hard, indivisible being, offered all naked to a vision which could be only total or null, but is rather a sort of straits between exterior horizons and interior horizons ever gaping open, something that comes to touch lightly and makes diverse regions of the colored or visible world resound at the distances, a certain differentiation, an ephe meral modulation of this world - *less a color or a thing, therefore than a difference between things and colors*. . .[30]

One conclusion of this analysis would be that the *ideality* that philosophers of language attribute to the *word* is mirrored in the ideality (or "invisibility" in one of the many imperfectly distinguished senses that Merleau-Ponty gives to this term) of what words themselves *refer to*. There simply is no such thing as an experience of "red" itself; every experience is of a "particular red thing" which is opposable to every other (qualitatively distinguishable) instance of what we would be disposed to take (for cultural reasons we hardly understand) as another "red" thing. In short, the experience of "red" (and of any other color) is always the experience of an instance or an example of "red," and thus it always implies the subunderstood rules which determine what is to count for us as an example of "red" and what is to be rejected as being "of another color." However fine the discriminations of the color adjectives of our natural language, or of our private idiolect of that language, we will never escape the component of ideality involved in our (culturally and intersubjectively determined) selective, perceptual perceiving of colors.

In short, the structures of perception are, for Merleau-Ponty, strict analogues of the structures of language. Colors are as "ideal" as phonemes: that is, the actual experiences of what we call red objects are to the color "red" what raw phonetics is to the ideal laws of phonemics. The phonemes (and the syntagmatic and paradigmatic rules of their opposability) that constitute the phonological system of any given natural language are, strictly *as phonemes*, not sounds at all. They are not the raw phonetic material which given historical speakers actually produce; they are, in fact, *never actually spoken, but only meant*.

Let me give my own example. If one utters the sound "p" in the English language, one *uses* the phoneme /p/. This /p/ may be aspirated, as in *pin*, or unaspirated, as in *spin*, since in English we do not distinguish (as some other languages do) between these two (aspirated and unaspirated) sounds which are potentially separate phonemes. One never does and one is never expected to produce on two separate occasions exactly the same phonetic sounds, the same raw phonetic material; this is neither necessary nor sufficient for understanding, and is, in any case, a physical impossibility. What is necessary and sufficient is that whatever is uttered, according to the syntagmatic and paradigmatic system of phonological opposables which are determined by the phonology of that language, *be meant and recognized as the same phoneme* which alone can hold that particular place in that particular phonological system. For instance, if someone speaking the English language systematically replaced the phoneme /p/ by the phoneme /b/, no matter how bad the accent, no matter how deformed the raw phonetic material, I will cease to have any difficulty at all in compensating for any number of various complex phonetic variations once I have grasped the abstract laws of this particular phonological system. Phonemes are not real sounds at all; they are, rather, the ideal elements which are opposable, according to rule, to all the other limited number of phonemes which constitute this particular language. It was Merleau-Ponty's belief that a similar structure of "diacritical, relative, oppositional" rules governs perception and all other forms of objectification, and this belief underlies his final and most mature attempt to relate the various orders of intentionality to one another.[31]

Even without further developing this pregnant analogy we see the astonishing development of Merleau-Ponty's original project which is here brought to the fore. Whereas he had originally begun with the very Husserlian thesis that linguistic meaning is "founded" in the perceptual articulation of objects, in his final work he was attempting to understand the perceptual articulation of the world on the analogy of linguistic structure. Nobody – not even Merleau-Ponty - could *know* whether this new and vastly more comprehensive investigation would provide us with a definitive theory of the proper way in which to interrelate the structures of "perceptual consciousness" and "linguistic consciousness," because he left us while still in the midst of thinking out his own first systematic statement of what such a task would involve.

I submit, therefore, that this central thread of his thought, which unites his final work to his earliest preoccupation with the thesis of the "primacy of perception," and the attempt to understand and articulate the phenomenological concept of *Fundierung* within a completed phenomenology of the experienced world, is the deepest basis for his continued and urgently *present* contemporary significance for philosophy, particularly because this is a task shared not only by phenomenologists but by all contemporary philosophers of language and the speech-act.

CHAPTER III

THE MEANING AND DEVELOPMENT
OF
MERLEAU-PONTY'S
CONCEPT OF STRUCTURE

Much of the most recent commentary on Merleau-Ponty's work concerns the development of his concept of structure and structuralism.[1] Many of the most recent commentators are particularly interested in revealing the common thread which they claim runs through his thought on structuralism from his earliest work to the end. These commentators nearly all divide Merleau-Ponty's development into three periods as I was myself at first content to do and did for the sake of economy in Chapter I of this book. But it is the thesis of this chapter that we need to distinguish four very distinct periods in his development on this question and, secondly, that the theories of structure developed in these four different periods are so distinct from one another as to be the possible bases for four completely distinct philosophical methodologies. It is my thesis that it is only during the third period (what I have elsewhere called the "middle" period) that he developed his ideas on linguistic structuralism in any strict sense.

Though there is an interest in language from his earliest work (*The Structure of Behavior* and *The Phenomenology of Perception*), there is no discussion of structuralism in the technical sense. It was only after the appearance of Sartre's book *What is Literature?* in 1947 that Merleau-Ponty's thought began to focus almost exclusively on language and linguistics.[2] In 1948 he gave an extensive first course on language at Lyon, a course that was repeated in much developed form at the Sorbonne in 1949 under the title *Consciousness and the Acquisition of Language*. During the following decade he was drawn more and more into the theory of language and literature. With his typical thoroughness he began with a survey of all the material then available on scientific linguistics, with special reference to Saussure. Thus, unlike his contemporaries in the Anglo-American philosophical world, who developed a theory of language based on speech-acts (Wittgenstein, Austin, Ryle, etc.) which totally ignores the contributions of scientific linguistics, Merleau-Ponty's reflections on language

are based directly on linguistic structuralism. During the period
from 1949 to 1953, the year of his inaugural lecture at the
Collège de France, his interest in language is almost exclusive.
As I have said elsewhere: from 1949 onward language began to
become the central preoccupation; it was no longer treated as just
one example among many of the specifically human institution of
meaning, but is now set up as the privileged mode of our experience of meaning of all kinds. The structures of perception, and even
gestalt presentations are interpreted in terms of the oppositive,
diacritical binary oppositions of phonology. Even color perception
is seen to be a matter of being immersed in a system of differences, analogous to those of language. In short, from being a
peripheral, though always important, consideration in his phenomenological investigations, *the analysis of language now takes the
central place*. In his inaugural address to the Collège de France
in 1953 he went so far as to credit Saussurean linguistics with
developing a "theory of signs" that could serve as a sounder basis
for the philosophy of history than the thought of either Marx or
Hegel, which he had primarily adopted in the works of his "prelinguistic" period. He did not, of course, believe (like
Wittgenstein) that the study of language alone would solve all
philosophical problems, but he did believe that linguistics would
give us the paradigm model on the basis of which he would be able
to elaborate a theory of the human sciences and thus establish a
universal, philosophical anthropology.[3]

However, from the commencement of his teaching at the Collège
de France he begins to doubt this new position and his thought
begins to move into a new and strikingly different direction. From
this year, 1953, he seems to have lost interest both in *The Prose
of the World*, the book on which he was then working, and his
project for a book on *The Origin of Truth*, and had completely
abandoned all interest in both these projects by 1959.[4] The
reasons for this abrupt and puzzling change of direction are
obscure though I will present my own hypothesis below. In any case
it is evident that the fourth and final period of his thought,
which begins around 1959, culminated in the difficult and obscure
reflections of *The Visible and the Invisible*, a work which was
meant to replace all the projects he had begun during the 1953-
1959 period.

1.   MERLEAU-PONTY AND LINGUISTIC STRUCTURALISM

As I have said, I distinguish four periods in the development
of Merleau-Ponty's concept of structure. These can be conveniently
labeled: (1) Gestaltist, (2) Dialectical, (3) Structuralist, and

(4) Post-Structuralist (in a specifically Merleau-Pontean, i.e., pre-Derridian, sense of "post-structuralism"). For the purpose of our discussion here it is best to begin with Merleau-Ponty's most highly developed discussions of structuralism and then return to his earliest work before going on to the final period.

His discovery of linguistic structuralism, he tells us, was primarily influenced by Saussure's theory of the linguistic sign.

> We have learned from Saussure that, taken singly, signs do not signify anything, and that each one of them does not so much express a meaning as mark a divergence of meaning between itself and other signs.[5]

> The well-known definition of the sign as "diacritical, oppositive, and negative" means that language is present in the speaking subject as a system of intervals between signs and significations, and that, as a unity, the act of speech simultaneously operates the differentiation of these two orders.[6]

In short, the scientific study of phonology shows us that natural languages are based on systems of binary oppositions according to which the recognized phonemes of a given language are opposable, according to rule, to all the other phonemes of that language. The "miracle" of language is that a restricted number of phonemes – which in themselves mean nothing – enable us to develop the whole world of discourse based on a highly restricted number of binary oppositions which provide us with the fundamental, formal rules of our language.

At the same time, and not surprisingly in view of his earlier phenomenology, it is not this aspect of linguistic theory which most interested Merleau-Ponty or held his attention. He was even less interested (until he was forced to face it in *The Prose of the World*) in the distinction between surface and depth grammar and, indeed, tried to avoid for as long as he could any notion of an "ideal grammar" underlying the surface string.[7] We will take up the reasons for this presently. For now, let us emphasize that one distinction which Merleau-Ponty took from Saussure, namely the distinction between *la langue* and *la parole*, *la langue* being the *rules* of language and *la parole* being the *acts* of speaking.

(1) First, in his course of 1949, *Consciousness and the Acquisition of Language*, *la langue* is defined as "a system of possibilities" whereas *la parole* is "what one says." *La langue* would therefore define the field of ideal possibilities for

expression and *la parole* would be the exercise of these possibilities. The dialectical difficulty - and this is what most fasci-
nates Merleau-Ponty - with this distinction is that *la langue*
itself follows a "kind of blundering logic" rather than the purely
conceptual logic of the proposition. *La langue* is to speech what
the body is to consciousness. The body, like language, follows a
"blind logic" which presents us with a "conventional" or
"cultural" system which is not based on any explicit common decision. We cannot, for instance, give an exact date to the time
when the Latin language become French though, as we follow the
diachronic evolution of this language, we may be able to note the
emergence over time of a certain "archetectonic" which is no
longer that of Latin. The unity of the system is not that of an
ideal grammar, in Merleau-Ponty's view, but of "the idea of a
unity of a language-function across languages. . . of a concrete
universality which realizes itself only gradually and finds itself
treating the expressive desire which animates languages rather
than the transitory forms which are its result."[8] French defines
itself in the present as the common aim of all subjects who speak
it to the extent that they are able to communicate among themselves. Language, therefore, is neither "a transcendent reality
with respect to all the speaking subjects" nor is it "a phantasm
formed by the individual."[9] It is rather the enigmatic point of
intersection of speaking and meaning which enables thought to be
articulated.[10] As Vendryes said: "Language is an ideal which can
be sought, but never found; a potential reality never actually
realized; a becoming which never comes."[11] The importance of
structuralist linguistics for Merleau-Ponty is to have put this
problem at the center though how it is to be solved, at this
stage, is unclear.

   (2) In the section on "Linguistics" in his essay on *Phenomenology and the Sciences of Man* (1951) Merleau-Ponty is more
dramatic: "But for the subject who is actually speaking, who is no
longer an *observer* confronting language as an *object*, his langauge
is undoubtedly a distinct reality. There are regions where he can
make himself understood and others where he cannot. . . the cir-
cumstances may be more or less precise, more or less rigorous,
more or less complex, depending upon the culture of the speaker.
But for him there is always a moment, a boundary, beyond which he
no longer understands and is no longer understood."[12]

   Clearly, Merleau-Ponty understands *la langue* exclusively in
terms of what linguists today call the "surface string" as opposed
to "deep structures." But, even so, *la langue* prescribes the
common rules according to which all must speak if they are to be
understood; language in this sense is correlative to and co-

extensive with acts of speaking. Language is not a thing but a
system of rules which subsists "in the air *between* the speaking
subjects but [is] never fully realized in any of them."[13]
    For the members of any natural linguistic community present
usage is independent of etymology and the past history of the
language. The speaking subject is turned towards the future.
Language is the intention of saying something about something to
somebody. No matter how "scientific" we may become there is "no
rigorous procedure which will enable us to determine the exact
beginning of a linguistic reality. It has no precise spatial and
temporal limits. . . [There is] no determinate place where
Provencal as a whole is perfectly realized. . . [in fact] there is
only a single language, since there is no way of finding the
precise limit where one passes into another."[14]

>   The language which is present, actual, and effective
>   becomes the model for understanding other possible modes of
>   speech. It is in our experience of speaking that we must find
>   the germ of universality which will enable us to understand
>   other languages.[15]

    Thus, in his discussions of the distinction between *la langue*
and *la parole* Merleau-Ponty throughout seems to give priority to
la parole which can only lead to difficulties when he later
attempts to stress the systematic and formal character of "sign
systems" as he does in *In Praise of Philosophy* (1953).
    There he writes, in a passage which is much more in the
strictly structuralist vein while retaining his usual rhetorical
eloquence:

>   Meaning lies latent not only in language, in political
>   and religious institutions, but in modes of kinship, in
>   machines, in the landscape, in production, and, in general,
>   in all the modes of human commerce. An interconnection among
>   all these phenomena is possible, *since they are all sym-
>   bolisms*, and perhaps even the translation of one symbolism
>   into another is possible.[16]

    (3) It was, indeed, in this inauguaral lecture of 1953 that
Merleau-Ponty summed up the central focus of his interest in
scientific linguistic structuralism:

>   The theory of signs as developed in linguistics. . .
>   implies a conception of historical meaning which gets beyond
>   the opposition of *things* versus *consciousness*. Living

language is precisely that togetherness of thinking and thing which causes the difficulty. In the act of speaking, the subject, in his tone and in his style, bears witness to his autonomy, since nothing is more proper to him, and yet at the same moment, and without contradiction, he is turned toward the linguistic community and is dependent on his language. The will to speak is one and the same as the will to be understood. The presence of the individual in an institution and of the institution in the individual is evident in the case of linguistic change. It is often the wearing down of a form which suggests to us a new way of using the means of discrimination which are present in the language at a given time. The constant need for communication leads us to invent and accept a new usage which is not deliberate and yet which is systematic. The contingent fact, taken over by the will to expression, becomes a new means of expression which takes its place, and has a lasting sense in the history of this language. In such cases, there is a rationality in the contingent, a lived logic, a self-constitution of which we have definite need in trying to understand the union of contingency and meaning in history. . .[17]

Readers of *The Visible and the Invisible* will not fail to foresee here the developments which later lead Merleau-Ponty to give up his attempt to use the structural analysis of language as the privileged method and model for the explanation of *all* experience and to reinsert it into experience as just one more manifestation of something more fundamental, namely the unity of *thing* and *consciousness* in some ineffable, inarticulable, unity which transcends all contradictions.

In short, what most interested Merleau-Ponty in the structuralist attempt to establish phonological, morphological and syntactical rules (which we call *la langue*) *according to which* we must speak in order to make sense, is the dialectual relationship of these rules or structures to actual acts of usage. On the one hand the structures of language are nothing other than the scientific description of speech acts, and therefore are ontologically dependent on a community of speakers. On the other hand this community of speakers must already – in some dumb, sub-understood manner – follow the rules of *la langue* even while their language patterns are being described. Here we have a good dialectical situation. Neither is prior to the other, neither can subsist without the other, neither is independent of the other. Each is necessary for the constitution of meaning and the articulation of thought. It is, I submit, Merleau-Ponty's attempt at a dialectical reconciliation of these two aspects of language which is at once the high point of his reflections on linguistic structuralism and at the same time the ruination of his structuralist-linguistic program. For, no sooner is this dialectical problem carefully stated – and it is stated again and again in the works of this period – than Merleau-Ponty abandons it. But before continuing our argument we must return to Merleau-Ponty's pre-structualist writings. I divide his conceptions in this period under two headings: the Gestaltist, and the Dialectical.

2. MERLEAU-PONTY'S EARLY THEORIES OF STRUCTURE

To bring a dialectical cast, even of exposition, to the phenomenological thought of Edmund Husserl would seem to be an audacious enterprise – given the fact both that the name of Hegel and the term "dialectic" are excluded from the writings of Husserl, by conscious design. From the very first page of the *Phenomenology of Perception* we are clearly in a new and strange phenomenological climate. But before going to the *Phenomenology of Perception* it is necessary to take a brief look at Merleau-Ponty's first major work, namely *The Structure of Behavior*, to examine the sense that he gives to the word "structure" there. The major source of the notion of structure developed in Merleau-Ponty's first book is that which was developed in gestalt psychology, which in turn was largely influenced by Husserl's *Third Investigation*, "The Logic of Parts and Wholes." This is the notion which defines the structure as being more than a simple combination of parts or elements, but rather the new reality which emerges from the special form in which a number of necessarily interdependent parts or elements combine in such wise that the whole would not be what it is if it were composed of different elements, nor would the elements which constitute a given whole be the same if they were to be found in a different whole or in isolation.

Whether one takes the route of conceptual analysis, as Husserl did in the *Third Investigation*, or bases oneself on the empirical results of Gestalt psychology, as Merleau-Ponty preferred to do, there are essentially two ways in which parts and wholes can be related. (1) There are wholes which are mere "aggregates," constituted of parts or elements which have no intrinsic connection with one another, no *reason* residing in themselves to be "taken together." (2) And then there are other "wholes" whose analysis into parts shows that the parts mutually interpenetrate one another and logically imply one another.

This latter serves as the basis for the notion of "structure" developed by such German thinkers as Rubin, Lewin, Metzgar, Koffka, Koehler, Gelb, Goldstein, and Gurwitsch. After Gurwitsch fled Germany in 1933 and established himself in Paris, Merleau-Ponty became his student and collaborator.[18] The bibliography with which Gurwitsch provided him, particularly in his famous article "Quelques aspects. . .de la psychologie de la forme," serves as the backbone for the investigations in *The Structure of Behavior*, even though Merleau-Ponty hardly recognizes the important influence of Gurwitsch on this book and on his thought as a whole. On the basis of this Gestaltist literature and the analysis it contains, Merleau-Ponty, in *The Structure of Behavior*, reinterprets the distinction between "the physical," "the biological," and "the mental" to show that biological (or vital) structures presuppose physical structures, and that mental structures presuppose both. They are not only *de facto* but *logically* cumulative in such wise that the higher, though it can never be reduced to the lower, necessary presupposes it. Hegel is hardly mentioned in this book; the entire analysis and argument is based, usually indirectly and through Gestalt theory, on Husserl's concept of *Fundierung*, an analysis of how higher forms of experience can be and necessarily must be *founded* on lower forms.

This early notion of structure is clearly not to be identified with that of linguistic structuralism, though interesting analogies can be formulated. There is certainly no evidence that the founders of linguistic structuralism, like Troubetskoy, Saussure, Jakobson, or their followers, were particularly influenced by Gestalt psychology (though they were influenced by Husserl's *Logical Investigations*). Their notion of structuralism arose quite independently of any psychological research. Nevertheless, later on, when Merleau-Ponty does develop his views on linguistic structuralism he finds it perfectly natural to describe language as "not a Gestalt of the moment, but a Gestalt in movement, evolving toward a certain equilbrium."[19]

What distinguishes the structure of the diachronic natural language from that of the Gestaltists is that the elements constituting the "structure" are not simply and statically *juxtaposed* but are dynamically developing in time. It is clear that anyone who would identify these two senses of structure would be making a serious equivocation. Raymond Boudon has rightly insisted on this point. However, it does not seem that he is fully justified in his extremely negative criticism of what might be taken to be the fumbling of Merleau-Ponty's early work. He writes in one place of Merleau-Ponty and Goldstein as follows:

Even though at their time the works of Merleau-Ponty and the French translation of *The Organism* were able to appear as revelations, one does not find in either of them any kind of theory of the organism or of behavior *as systems*, but only a passionately interesting collection of observations. No doubt these observations show that an organism reacts as a whole and that a behavior cannot be understood except as a whole. But who could ever have doubted such banalities? [20]

There is a certain fluidity, lack of contour, perhaps a deliberate inexactitude, vagueness, and ambiguity in Merleau-Ponty's early definition of structure, but it does not seem that the originality of his work can be summarily dismissed. On the other hand it is clear that, as Merleau-Ponty developed, he radically changed his definition of "structure" at each step.

In any case what is added in Merleau-Ponty's second major work, *The Phenomenology of Perception* is a new and different concept of "structure" - a notion greatly influenced by his own idiosyncratic reading of Hegel. What distinguishes *The Phenomenology of Perception* from Merleau-Ponty's first book is the highly dialectical style of exposition it employs (something nowhere found in *The Structure of Behavior*). Though Merleau-Ponty continues to speak the language of Husserl and Gurwitsch in developing the eidetic structures of perceptual consciousness, and its embodiment, his writing takes on a very heavy Hegelian tone - something which Husserl would certainly have disavowed. Moreover, and secondly, when he treats of language in this book, there is no mention of Saussure or of structural linguistics. He is still completely innocent of these authors. Language is treated as but one aspect of the total bodily organization in the primary field of experience as one more aspect of the expressive and gestural constitution of meaning which Merleau-Ponty orchestrates in this book. [21]

The dialectical cast of his interpretation of Husserlian phenomenology is evident from the first sentences of the Introduction. He gives a "Hegelian" interpretation of the four central concepts of Husserl's phenomenology: namely, the concept of the reduction to experience, of the experience of other persons in "transcendental intersubjectivity," the notions of fact and essence, and the notion of intentionality. The phenomenological reduction, we read, is both possible and impossible at one and the same time; there is a truth of solipsism and a truth of intersubjectivity and both must be maintained in their opposed balance. Every fact is the instantiation of an essence and yet no fact can exhaust the essence; the world of experience can both be known and at the same time not known, eidetically. Consciousness is a "project of the world" which transcends itself towards what it is not and never will be, and consciousness is, at the same time, the "pre-objective" possession of itself in immanence. Consciousness, in short, is both transcendent and immanent, at the same time.

It seems that Merleau-Ponty took his notion of dialectics from two major sources, first of all from the teaching of Kojève, whose specialized and "existential" interpretation of Hegel made the members of Merleau-Ponty's student-generation for the first time fully conversant with Hegel. Merleau-Ponty is strongly influenced by the strong equivocation which pervades Kojeve's interpretation insofar as he seems almost to identify the sense of "phenomenology" in *The Phenomenology of Mind* with Husserl's phenomenology. This bringing together of Husserl and Hegel as contributors to *one* new kind of phenomenology is characteristic of the French phenomenology not only of Merleau-Ponty but also of Sartre.

The second source of Merleau-Ponty's dialectical notions comes mostly from Marx, and was no doubt highly influenced by his leftist political interests and his special interest in the philosophy of history and culture.

He wrote in *Sense and Nonsense*:

. . . all the great philosophical ideas of the past century – the philosophy of Marx and Nietzsche, phenomenology, German existentialism, and psychoanalysis – had their beginnings in Hegel; it was he who started the attempt to explore the irrational integrated into an expanded reason which remains the task of our century. He is the inventor of that Reason, broader than the understanding, which can respect the variety and singularity of individual consciousness, civilization, ways of thinking, and historical contingency but which nevertheless does not give up the attempt to master them in order to guide to their own truth.[22]

In the light of this and similarly strong statements on the importance of Hegel's dialectical method it is all the more impressive to note, once again, that in 1953 – with his discovery of linguistic structuralism – he states that the Saussurean theory of the sign will supplant both Marx and Hegel. Thus we cannot doubt that, in the development of his own thought, there is a strong contrast between Merleau-Ponty's earliest concepts of structure and those we have presented as the discoveries of the years 1947–1953 when he dedicated himself to an enthusiasm for linguistics which, at least in its verbal expression, as well as in its fate in his future thought, sometimes seems embarrassing. There are

clearly themes and ideas which go through Merleau-Ponty's corpus
as a whole - ideas which come up again and again in different
guises. There is thus a "unity" to his project as a whole. What
is, however, not unified and completely distinct are the four
senses of "structure" and the four methods he developed to deal
with it at each of the four turning-points of his career.

3. MERLEAU-PONTY'S FINAL, POST-STRUCTURALIST, PERIOD

Given the strength of his convictions concerning the importance of linguistic structuralism for the explanation of human
behavior and all that he wrote about the matter in the decade
1949-1959, it is puzzling to all of his readers that he should
have so abruptly and completely abandoned this structuralism in
his final work. As we have noted he left *The Prose of the World*
incomplete, and totally abandoned his plan to write on *The Origin
of Truth* - which was to have been, in his own words, the crown of
his philosophical career.[23] Instead, from around 1959 until the
time of his death he began working on a series of studies now
entitled *The Visible and the Invisible*. This work, far from ever
having been completed,[24] comes down to us in the form of a half-
written treatise - directed mainly against Sartrean ontology - and
an unfinished and disordered mass of working notes. For better or
for worse there are a number of contemporary writers who take the
development of the ideas in *The Visible and the Invisible* to be a
rectilinear development and final culmination of the major thrust
of his work from the very beginning. Some of these writers go
further to find a thread which unites Merleau-Ponty's thought as
it developed through these various stages in terms of what they
call a "structural ontology." It does not seem to me that this can
be correct for the simple reason that the sense of "structure"
which one can glean from a reading of *The Visible and the Invisible* has only a tenuous relationship to his earlier notions.
Two points must be made.

(1) The first point concerns Merleau-Ponty's dialectical
method which is more and more emphasized, and which becomes more
and more obscure as his work on *The Visible and the Invisible*
progresses. About the only thing that is truly clear is that in
his concept of dialectic, unlike that of Hegel but like that of
Sartre,[25] there is no room for and no necessity of any dialectical
reconciliation between opposites, in short no *synthesis*. His is a
dialectic which holds contradictories together in a never stable
and always temporally evolving disequilibrium. Always the "philo-

sopher of ambiguity," in his final period Merleau-Ponty becomes
the philosopher of contradiction.

Any commentator who adopts as a heuristic principle the rule
that one must explain the obscure passages in an author by the
passages on the same subject in which he expresses himself clearly, will not attempt to interpret his early works, whether in-
spired by Gestalt psychology, by dialectics, or by linguistic
structuralism, in terms of the argumentation of *The Visible and
the Invisible,* [26] for this would be to interpret what is clearly
said by what is obscure and, ultimately, to give no interpretation
at all. For, it is not at all evident that the guiding principle
for the interpretation of the thought of a philosopher ought to be
that his thought improves, matures, and gets better as he grows
older. If such a principle were to be universally adopted, we
would find ourselves interpreting Kant's *Critique of Pure Reason*
in terms of the obscure mystical of the *Opus Posthumum.* There is
certainly no apriori reason to suppose that the rambling and
sometimes incoherent positions taken in the working notes of *The
Visible and the Invisible* ought to be granted a special place in
the interpretation of Merleau-Ponty's thought as a whole.

(2) This brings us to the second and more important point,
namely that of an interpretation of the "binary" yet "dialectical"
opposition of the "visible" and the "invisible," which he says
pervades and constitutes the entire field of "Being."

It is not clear that the various oppositions which Merleau-
Ponty sets up binding and dividing the "visible" and the "invisible" together are dialectical, at least in the Hegelian sense.
It would seem more just to interpret them like a Heraclitean
identification of opposites held together in their contradictori-
ness at one and the same time.

When we first begin to make a list of the things Merleau-
Ponty means by the "visible" and the "invisible" we are reassured
that they should be able to be phenomenologically elucidated:

1. The perception of objects which are not, strictly
speaking, given to me in perceptual presentation, but which I
nevertheless perceive, such as "objects behind my back."

2. The experience of imagining absences, possibilities,
potentialities, contingencies, counter-factual conditionals,
the subjunctive, the optative, etc.

3. The perception of others insofar as the perception of
the other presents a body (surface) in which there is a (non-
spatial) mind, the body being "visible," the mind being

"invisible" (in the sense of the Husserlian appresented object). The experience of my own mind in my own body which is "posterior" to the experience of embodiment.

4. The silence which surrounds language, as *la langue* "precedes" and surrounds *la parole*.[27]

5. Consciousness and Unconsciousness.

6. The Husserlian distinction between fact and essence.

7. The relationship between the present state of a science which is moving towards a more perfect stage of the same science, which will be recognizably the *same* science, though it does not yet exist. Etc.

If this were all that Merleau-Ponty meant by the opposition of the "visible" and the "invisible," we could all heave a sigh of relief, for we are on familiar ground. And, no doubt, he does have a universal synthesis of such oppositions in mind and wants to show forth their "ground." The question, then, is about the methodology for reaching this ground or ultimate foundation (in "Being" with a capital *B*). It certainly is not Gestaltist; it certainly is not phenomenological; it certainly is not structuralist; is it dialectical?

Many obscure works have been written about this and, in the absence of a full study of the development of Merleau-Ponty's concept of dialectics, we must limit ourselves to a few observations. The Being which is revealed by this dialectic is a Being which is never wholly itself, that is what it is, and thus is the foundation of its own truth and meaning (there is *no distinction* between meaning and truth in Merleau-Ponty by this time) but whose meaning and truth transcend it. Its internal relations are both *necessary* and *incompatible.*

An absolute negativism – that is, one that thinks the negative is its originality – and an absolute positivism – that is, one that thinks being in its plenitude and its self-sufficiency – are exactly synonymous; there is not the least divergence between them.[28]

When one suggests that, in his final period, Merleau-Ponty may have ushered in the age of "post-structuralism," one evokes the frightening thought of Derridianism, and one must be fair. But the central question such thinkers, including Merleau-Ponty must be held to answer is whether their sense of dialectics - unlike the classical sense - requires not only the abandonment of any theory of the transcendental presuppositions of formal logic (since there can no longer be a transcendental, i.e. experiential, foundation of anything) but of formal logic itself. We have learned in contemporary debate that the most instructive question which can be posed to a person who professes to hold a dialectical logic is whether or not this dialectical logic supplants and erases the need for a formal logic. If the answer is "yes," we know the man is not only not a very good logician, but that he is also not a very good Platonist or Hegelian. Certainly the Derridean poststructuralists and deconstructionists speak and write in this manner,[29] and it is for this reason that one can, in reading Merleau-Ponty's final work, pose the question of his responsibility for it.

However, in all fairness to Merleau-Ponty, we must note that one of the difficulties in reading his last work is that, except when he is arguing with Sartre, he makes very few theoretical claims at all. Instead, we have a plethora of fascinating examples, cast up in a prolific and often chaotic profusion: Since each individual perceives his own world, the common world (*koinos kosmos*) is not perceived; yet, still, it is perceived. My hand has to be felt from the inside at the same time it is felt from the outside, and seeing is also a kind of touching of things with our look. The body sees the world but it also experiences itself being seen by things - the experience of painters, in which Merleau-Ponty was so interested - to the point that one is no longer able to say who sees and who is seen.

> . . . it is not I who sees, not *he* who sees, because an anonymous visibility inhabits both of us, a vision in general, in virtue of that primordial property that belongs to the flesh, being here and now, of radiating everywhere and forever, being an individual, of being also. . . universal.[30]

Until we reach what could be, or could have been, the culminating apostrophe of his final thought:

> There is an experience of the visible thing as preexisting my vision, but this experience is not a fusion, a coincidence; because my eyes which see, my hands which touch, can also be seen and touched, because, therefore, in this

sense they see and touch the visible, the tangible, from
within. . . . the world and I are within one another and
there is no anteriority of the *percipere* over the *percipi*,
there is simultaneity or even retardation.[31]

No philosopher of experience can help but stand in awe of
Merleau-Ponty's uncanny ability to describe the fine nuances of
perceptual experience, an ability in this regard greater even than
that of William James. *It is the philosophical method behind it
that is in question.* What are we to make of these statements
methodologically? Is this dialectical argument? Is "anteriority"
in this passage to be understood in a logical sense? In a temporal
sense? In an ontological sense? Answers to questions of this kind
appear nowhere. One thing is certain: if there is no "anteriority"
of the *percipere* in *any* sense, we have abandoned phenomenology. No
matter that the "there is" of Being can be called "the intersection of being," "reversibility," "chiasm," "flesh," even
"savage flesh." It is not that these metaphors cannot be understood or that they are not extremely (often misleadingly) evoca-
tive. But what is the (philosophical) *method* for the investigation
of this "Being"? Can it be called "structuralist" in any sense
that will yield a "structural ontology"? Though some commentators
say so, it is not clear that Merleau-Ponty does.

4. CONCLUSION

But to the extent that we are mainly interested in the *evolution* and *development* of his thought, we are not so much interested
in the question of whether or not his last work involves either a
return to an earlier concept of dialectics, or the development of
a new concept. Albert Rabil[32] tells us that during the years 1945–
50 (therefore, though Rabil does not say so, during the period of
his discovery of linguistic structuralism) Merleau-Ponty decided
to abandon his earlier "dialectic." Whether or not this is true we
are not certain, and must propose a hypothesis. The main question
we are interested in here is *why* certainly after 1959, and perhaps
as early as 1953, he abandoned all work on *The Prose of the World*
and took up the obscure reflections which finally emerged in *The
Visible and the Invisible.*

My hypothesis is based on an examination of those passages in
The Prose of the World in which, in spite of himself, Merleau-
Ponty is required by the logic of his own investigations into
language to recognize and find a place for the algorithmic and
formally logical structures of language.[33] If, of course, he had
been able to study the (later) linguistics of scholars like Zellig

Harris or Noam Chomsky, instead of the much more primitive and underdeveloped literature available to him, he would not, perhaps, have been so long able to ignore the universal apriori structures of deep grammar or spend so much argument attempting to show that the *only* "universal" characteristics of language come about from the "oblique passage," or the "lateral transfer" that occurs between one surface structure and another.

Certainly, it would seem that the kind of binary oppositions presupposed in the very foundations of phonology and linguistic structuralism in general, the only logic the computer can use, the only logic in which linguists like Chomsky, for instance, would be interested, is too closely dependent on the law of non-contradiction as it is formulated in formal logic (as well as in the transcendental critique of formal logic)[34] for Merleau-Ponty to find it congenial.

It is as if he came to see this pitfall of linguistic structuralism only little by little. It is as if when, finally forced by a deeper reading of structural linguistics, he saw that he was going to have to abandon or modify his earlier "Gestaltist" and "dialectical" interpretation of linguistic structuralism, he abandoned it. Not much more can be said. There are those, like myself, who (since we believe the method of linguistic structuralism will provide us with a model and method for explanation in the human sciences with far more explanatory power than any method presently in use) would have found a further and newer development of Merleau-Ponty's structuralism a positive advance in his thought. There are no doubt others who find his return to or creation of an opposed "dialectical" method an advance also. The important point in either case requires the recognition of the shifting senses in which he used the term "structure" in the various periods of his philosophical development and the recognition that there is no rectilinear development of any single, clearly delineated and well-defined concept of structure or structuralism which runs through his thought from beginning to end.

CHAPTER IV

MERLEAU-PONTY:

THE TRIUMPH OF DIALECTICS

OVER STRUCTURALISM

It is truly astonishing that not one of the numerous commentators on the thought of Merleau-Ponty, not even those who have been concerned with his philosophy of language, have given much serious attention to the pivotal work in his development, namely *The Prose of the World*. This work is, of course, devoted primarily to the philosophy of language, which was not at all stages of his development at the center of his philosophical investigations. Nevertheless, from the years 1949 to roughly 1953 it was the question of language which was at the center of his preoccupations. Moreover, if we go back to the period shortly after he took up teaching at the Sorbonne in Paris, and when he presented his candidacy for the chair of philosophy at the Collège de France, he described the work on this book. *The Prose of the World*, as being an integral part, perhaps the most important part, of the future culmination of his philosophical career.[1]

Of course, one of the reasons for the neglect of this work and the failure to see its pivotal importance in his development was that he himself abandoned it and did not permit its publication during his lifetime. It was only eight years after his death that Claude Lefort finally put it together as best he could and had it published.[2] But if we approach the work of Merleau-Ponty from a methodological point of view we see that the period that begins around 1949, when he completed *Consciousness and the Acquisition of Language*, marked a crisis or turning point in his development, a crisis that culminated in the anguish of *The Prose of the World*. Here begins the battle between dialectics and structuralism in his own mind and work. We will try to describe this battle up to the point at which it was resolved by the complete triumph of dialectics and the abandonment of structuralism as a method.

However, before going directly to what we call the battle between dialectics and structuralism in his thought, we should take a methodological look at his early prestructuralist writings. In his first major book, *The Structure of Behavior*, there is certainly no structuralism nor is there strictly speaking any dialectic. Hegel is mentioned but is not prominent. The main sources are Husserl and gestalt psychology, particularly as interpreted by Aron Gurwitsch.[3] The notion of "structure" developed in this book is definitely that of a developed and dynamic gestalt theory applied not only to perception but to the scientific theory of perception and to behavior in general. In this book he reinterprets the distinction between "the physical," "the biological," and "the mental" to show that biological (or vital) structures presuppose physical structures, and that mental structures presuppose both. They are not only empirically but logically cumulative in such wise that the higher structures, though they can never be reduced to the lower, necessarily presuppose them.

The argument is subtle and foundational but it would be difficult to call it dialectical and there is happily in this first book no indication of his unfortunate later tendency of conflating Husserl and Hegel so as to assume (without argument) that their two phenomenologies are convergent if not the same thing.

The Structure of Behavior was completed in 1938 even though it was not published until 1942. By the time we come to the publication three years later, in 1945, of the *Phenomenology of Perception* Merleau-Ponty's methodology has clearly taken a new turn. That is a turn in the dialectical direction and which gives us from the very first page of the *Preface* the method of his early dialectic. He begins with a discussion of the central concepts of Husserl's phenomenology to show that each of these four central concepts in fact contains an antinomy. There is the concept of the reduction to experience, the concept of the experience of other persons in "transcendental intersubjectivity," the concept of the notions of fact and essence, and the concept of the notion of intentionality. His discussions of these antinomies, which underly phenomenology in his view, is anything but Husserlian, at least on the surface. The phenomenological reduction, he says, is both possible and impossible at one and the same time. There is a truth of solipsism and a truth of intersubjectivity and both must be maintained in their opposed balance. Every fact is the instantiation of an essence and yet no fact can exhaust its essence. The world of experience can be known and at the same time not known; its evidence is eidetically certain but only "presumptively" true. Consciousness is a "project of the world" which transcends itself towards what it is not and will never be, and yet consciousness is, at one and the same time, the "pre-objective" possession of itself in immanence. Consciousness is that ambiguous, paradoxical, and dialectical reality which is both transcendent and immanent at once.

I believe that the root of the dialectical method developed in the phenomenology of perception is not, however, to be found primarily in Merleau-Ponty's reflections on either Husserl or Hegel, but in his own studies of perception as these relate to the entire philosophical tradition, namely to the theories of perception that we find in Descartes, Spinoza, Leibniz, Lachelier, Lagneau, Alain, Hume, Berkeley, Kant and above all in more recent gestalt psychology and behaviorism. Here his method in each chapter is to oppose intellectualism (rationalism, idealism, spiritualism) and empiricism (realism, naturalism, positivism) to show in as elegant a dialectical manner as possible that both opposed theories contain a good deal of truth and to show that in some sense each is acceptable, but only when corrected by the other. The phenomenological truth of the matter always lies in elucidating and formulating that position which commits the mistakes of neither intellectualism nor empiricism, while preserving what is true in each. In his argument Merleau-Ponty attempts to show as elegantly as he can that each of these opposed theories on the matters discussed (e.g.. perception, attention, memory, motility, affectivity, speaking, thinking, etc.) fails for the same reason, and at that point phenomenology steps in to show why both are wrong and how a description of lived experience will bring us to the truth. The major difference between *The Structure of Behavior* and *The Phenomenology of Perception* in this regard is that whereas *The Structure of Behavior* dealt with scientific theories *about* perception, *The Phenomenology of Perception* always brings us back to direct perceptual experience itself, our primordial "having" of a world.

Now, after Merleau-Ponty began to read scientific linguistics in preparation for his deeper study of language, which we date around 1947, a serious upheaval in his thought occurred. On the one hand he had been working on the philosophy of history in the explicit context of Hegel and Marx and now he finds a method which can have nothing whatever to do with dialectical logic, that of linguistic structuralism, but which has greater explanatory power and which is much more illuminative of the phenomenon of language than anything dialectics can give us.

It is a pity that Noam Chomsky (i.e. the theory of transformational, generative grammar) did not arrive earlier on the scene. Chomsky is certainly a linguist with whom a phenomenologist *ought* to be able to argue. If Merleau-Ponty could have known Chomsky's more empirical discovery of the distinction between surface and depth grammar, he might not have been able to maintain his rejection of the distinction. Both Wittgenstein and Russell had seen that it was necessary to distinguish depth from surface grammar though they provided no theory to account for the distinction. Merleau-Ponty was, of course, well acquainted with Husserl's *Fourth Investigation* in which, using apriori and conceptual arguments, Husserl gives a complete theory of pure grammar as the first level of formal logic, a depth grammar coercive on all natural languages. Though Merleau-Ponty was never able to accept Husserl on this point he does, in his linguistic writings of the years 1949-1959, recognize its affinities with linguistic structuralism, and it is this very affinity which troubles him. He glories in his new discovery of structuralism but does not want to be constrained to return to the notion of a universal (depth) grammar common to all natural languages.[4] That would be too high a price to pay. His phenomenological theory of the body as expressive and communicative of thought shows forth a fundamental incompatibility with structuralism. And this caused him the intellectual anguish which finally made him give up the completion and the publication of *The Prose of the World*.

If I may be permitted a short digression I would like to remark that around this very time (1949) there clearly emerges a certain tension in Merleau-Ponty's conception of the relation of dialectics to a philosophy of history. In *Humanism and Terror* (published in the same year that he took his linguistic turn) amidst a number of interesting, provocative, and stimulating analyses, he makes such irrepressible and irresponsible statements as the following: Marxism is not just *one* philosophy of history, it is *the only* philosophy of history.

> Marxism is not just any hypothesis that might be replaced tomorrow by some other, it is the simple statement of those conditions without which there would be neither any humanism. . . nor any rationality in history. In this sense Marxism is not a philosophy of history; it is *the* philosophy of history.[5]

Whereas, in roughly the same time period, he states with the great enthusiasm he had during the year in which he assumed the chair of philosophy at the Collège de France that the linguistic structuralism of Saussure will provide us with a much sounder basis for the philosophy of history than the thought of either Hegel or Marx.[6]

In his 1952 paper addressed to the Collège de France (to support his candidacy for the chair of philosophy) he explains the relationship of his first two early works, *The Structure of Behavior* and *The Phenomenology of Perception*, to the work he has been doing since 1947-49. He gives a brief summary of his earlier work, and then says that in a series of further studies which he has undertaken since 1945, and which will definitely fix the philosophical significance of the earlier works, he is turning to language. In his first works he had studied the body-mind problem, the incarnation of subjectivity in the world. Now he will show that every incarnate subject "is like an open-notebook in which we do not yet know what will be written. . . .it is like a new language. . ."[7] In turning towards the study of language he is turning from the realm of our perceptual-motor insertion in the world, and the structures it enables us to achieve, to "the field of knowledge properly so-called." There are then two tasks before him: (1) a theory of truth, and (2) a theory of intersubjectivity. These tasks will be achieved in two books on the theory of truth, namely *The Prose of the World* and *The Origin of Truth*. He states clearly, even in this very preliminary study, what will turn out to be the major problem and ultimate stumbling-block of his whole investigation of language.

Language leads us to a thought which is no longer ours alone, to a thought which is presumptively universal, though this is never the universality of a pure concept which would be identical for every mind. It is rather the call which a situated thought addresses to other thoughts, equally situated, and each one responds to the call with its own resources. An examination of the domain of the algorithm would show here too, I believe, the same strange function which is at work in the so-called inexact forms of language. . . thought is never more than relatively formal.[8]

The problem that is here stated very vaguely in this preliminary way is the problem which he found himself ultimately unable to solve. On the one hand the idea of history, as a single history, of a logic of history, is implied in "the least human exchange, in the least social perception." Or to put it in other words, "the least use of language implies an idea of truth. . . our life is essentially universal."[9] But, on the other hand, since Merleau-Ponty will never fully agree to the structuralist requirement that the laws of language are foundational and universally valid for *any* and *every* natural language, he states that his method is only a "methodological" rationalism which must not be confused with a "dogmatic rationalism."[10]

For our purposes here it is irrelevant that he never proceeded beyond his conception of this work to its final culmination in *L'Homme transcendental* a work which he said would be a metaphysics and which would at the same time give us the principle of an ethics – because this work was not only never written but never even begun. We are now going to show *why* it was never written, what his stumbling block was, and therefore why he abandoned *The Prose of the World* only half completed, gave up all hope of writing *L'Origine de la verite*, and instead began amassing the notes for his final work, *The Visible and the Invisible*, which represents a complete abandonment of the project he presented to the Collège de France in 1952.

After finishing his first two works, *The Structure of Behavior* and the *Phenomenology of Perception*, as early as 1947 Merleau-Ponty began to read the writings of scientific linguistics and structuralism. He gave his first course on the philosophy of language in 1947 and 1948 at the University of Lyon and developed this course to be given at the Sorbonne the following year (1949) in the form we have of it as *Consciousness and the Acquisition of Language*. For approximately ten years, from 1949 to about 1959, Merleau-Ponty multiplied his writings on linguistic philosophy and linguistic structuralism, almost to the exclusion of everything else, even his dialectical predilections. All of the work was meant to culminate in *The Prose of the World*. During this period he frequently states his belief that the study of language is *the central* problem of philosophy, that even the phenomenology of perception must be understood in terms of the structures of language. [11]

Merleau-Ponty's earliest philosophy of language, as presented in his first two works, had been completely innocent of linguistic structuralism. In the context of his theory of perception and the embodiment of consciousness, he developed a gestural theory of language which was quite unique and which he never fully abandoned, nor had to abandon, in his later writings on language. What he did was to modify and reinterpret it in terms of the linguistic structuralism which he began to espouse from 1949 on.

But it must also be remarked that his understanding of and espousal of linguistic structuralism was of a very special kind, and was guided – even in spite of himself – by the dialectical preoccupation of the *Phenomenology of Perception*. In fact what most interested Merleau-Ponty about the philosophy of language was primarily the dialectical relationship between spoken language (*la parole*) and the fixed structures of language (*la langue*). He presented numerous explanations of this dialectical problem in the course of his writings on language – explanations which culminate in *The Prose of the World*.

That book begins with a very short, and enigmatic, not to say strange, chapter entitled "The Spectre of a Pure Language."

Without saying so he here introduces us immediately to his own central problem. On the one hand he was well familiar with Husserl's theory of language, Husserl's theory of the distinction between depth and surface grammar, Husserl's theory of pure apriori grammar, Husserl's theory of the scientific text, and so on. Yet at the same time he not only found it impossible to accept this foundational, universalistic theory of language and grammar, but felt obligated to show that Husserl himself abandoned, or at least began to abandon, this theory of universal grammar in his later writings. Already in his famous article "On the Phenomenology of Language" (1951)[12] he makes (without evidence) the astonishing claim that in his final works Husserl abandoned the theory of pure apriori grammar, *die reine Formenlehre der Bedeutungen.* This is certainly not true. In other texts of that period such as "Phenomenology and the Sciences of Man," Merleau-Ponty recognizes that he has been "pushing Husserl further than he wanted to go"[13] but justifies *his* presentation of the phenomenology of language in its relation to linguistics as justified by its intrinsic truth and its final solution of the problem of the relationship between spoken language and its intransigent and objectively coercive formal roles. What, then, is the problem?

From the point of view of structural linguistics, one would say that the major difficulty Merleau-Ponty faces is his unwillingness or inability to recognize any level of language deeper than the surface string. He considers language to be not only primarily but even exclusively a matter of communication. From his first writings he inserts language into the lived tissue of life-world experience and since communication occurs on levels much more fundamental than the spoken word or sentence, on the level of bodily gestures and expressions, he inserts language into these behaviors and interprets it in terms of them. The only "universality" he will accept in language is the ability of speakers of natural languages to make themselves intelligible, little by little, to one another. This is an "existential" or "affective" universality, not the logical substructure demanded by Husserl. The logical apriories of pure grammar are ruled out in favor of the "oblique" or "lateral" universality of the incomplete but sufficient comprehensibility which we effect in actually speaking to others. Since it is impossible to determine either geographically or in historical time where and when one dialect (or idiolect) ceases to merge into another, when any natural language ceases to be understood by those we take to be speaking "a different language," we can only say – at the limit – that there is only *one* language "in a state of becoming."[14]

I would be the last to attempt to denigrate Merleau-Ponty's great achievements in his descriptions of the speech act (*la parole*) and the existential communication which language enables us to achieve and which is an accomplishment of living-in-the-world prior to thought and knowledge. But there is the fact that over and above communication, or one might say as its *logical presupposition*, language serves to clarify our thoughts, to articulate what is only dumbly understood on the level of life-world experience. This is the level of what Merleau-Ponty in his memorandum of 1952 to the Collège de France recognized as the claim of knowledge and universal truth.

It is these two aspects of language which come into conflict in his attempt to reconcile *la parole* and *la langue* dialectically on the level of immediate, lived experience. It is as if in his early readings in scientific linguistics, and in particular in the contributions to phonology made by Saussure, (and his followers, predecessors and associates) Merleau-Ponty never fully recognized or appreciated the fact that phonology, and hence all of contemporary linguistics relies on a binary logic (the only kind of logic a computer, for instance, can use). The whole system of phonological oppositions in all natural languages is based on the possibility of the speakers of those languages being able to recognize sounds emitted as noises from the vocal apparatus of native speakers as opposable, according to rule, in binary fashion, to all the other sounds recognized as standing for phonemes in those languages. This, he could hardly have missed, but it took a good deal of time for it to sink in. When, later on, he was faced with the prospect of the necessity of choosing between structuralism and a dialectical description of lived experience, it was structuralism which he rejected.

But he had first of all tried to incorporate it into his own program. What was it that most of all interested Merleau-Ponty in structuralism?

To be brief, as we sift through his linguistic articles, it was, first of all (1) the "negative, diacritical, oppositive" value – the only value – it gives to linguistic signs. Linguistic signs, beginning with phonemes, in themselves mean nothing, signify nothing. It is only in combinations in which they are contrasted according to rule to other signs that they can signify. This fits in very well with Merleau-Ponty's theory of perception in which the positive is never positive except with the negative and the negative is negative only through the positive. Just as there is no "visible" without the "invisible," there is no speech without silence.

Which brings us to the second point of his interest (2), namely the discovery that the primary sense of "silence" within which the speech-act, the real, present act of making oneself understood (*la parole*), takes place, occurs only on the background of *la langue*, that is on the basis of all the subunderstood formal rules which enable speech to occur. Phenomenology studies the act of speaking; Structuralism studies the pre-supposed rules. The two, he claims, can be related dialectically.

In short, what most interested Merleau-Ponty in the structuralist attempt to establish phonological, morphological and syntactical rules (which we call *la langue*) *according to which* we must speak in order to make sense, is what he explained as the dialectical relationship of these rules or structures to actual acts of usage, to speech acts. On the one hand the structures of language are nothing other than the scientific description of speech acts, and therefore are ontologically dependent on a community of speakers. On the other hand this community of speakers must already - in some dumb, subunderstood manner - follow the rules of *la langue* even while their language patterns are being described. Here we have a perfect dialectical relationship. Neither is prior to the other, neither can subsist without the other, neither is independent of the other. Each is necessary for the constitution of meaning and the articulation of thought. But if I focus on one, the other disappears into the background at the expense of the other. They cannot both be brought into focus at the same time and in the same respect. It is in his reflections on this paradox of Structuralism, in this interpretation, that his philosophy of language reaches its high point and at the same time its ruination. For once this dialectical solution to the linguistic problem is stated - and it is stated again and again in the writings that lead up to *The Prose of the World* - Merleau-Ponty abandons it.

What Merleau-Ponty did not at first grasp in his early readings of structuralist literature was the extent to which it was necessarily tied to a binary logic, a computer logic, and that the very presence of "the algorithmic" in language undermines and challenges all dialectical logic, all dialectical solutions.

For purposes of brevity I here pinpoint that unpleasant discovery in *The Prose of the World*. The clue to Merleau-Ponty's abandonment of structuralism in favor of a new and more radical dialectical method (aimed at putting us in touch with our experience of *Being*) is to be found in the two principal chapters

of the book which he had announced in 1952 so confidently as
destined to be the culmination of his philosophical work, and
which he completely abandoned by 1959 in favor of something he had
not even dreamt of earlier.   I mean the chapters on "Science and
the Experience of Expression" and "The Algorithm and the Mystery
of Language" in *The Prose of the World*. In his earliest philosophy
of language in *The Phenomenology of Perception*, (in chapter 6 on
the Body as Expression and Speech) he had argued, in complete
innocence and ignorance of structural linguistics, for a gestural
theory of meaning. He tried several times to incorporate this very
interesting theory of language into his struc-turalist writings of
the period of the 1950's.

Now in *The Prose of the World*, when he is finally constrained
to give its due to the algorithmic character of language, he sees
that his gestural, affective, and existential theory of language
will be undermined. The essential distinction is that between
language as an instrument for immediate life-world communication
and language as an instrument of knowledge. He would like to be
able to reduce the latter to the former but structuralism does not
permit him to do so. We here have a crisis of understanding and a
cry of revolt. He writes:

It is not our purpose here to question the character of
truth which distinguishes the propositions of exact science
or the incomparability of the moment when, in recognizing a
truth, I touch on something that did not begin with me and
will not cease to signify after me. This experience of an
event which suddenly becomes hollow, losing its opacity,
revealing a transparence, and becoming forever a meaning as a
constant in culture and speech. . . . More precisely, one
cannot discover whether, even in exact science, there exists
between the institutionalized sign, and the *true*
significations they designate, an instituting speech which is
the vehicle of everything. When we say that the newly
discovered properties of a mathematical entity are as old as
it is, these very terms, "property" and "entity" already
contain an interpretation of our experience of truth. . . The
development of knowledge moves toward the totality of a
meaning. That is true. But essence conceived as the future of
knowledge is not an essence; it is what we call a structure.
Its relation to effective knowledge is like the relation of a
thing perceived to perception. Perception, which is an event,
opens on to the thing perceived, which appeared to be prior
to perception and to be true before it. . . .

> We are not reducing mathematical evidence to perceptual
> evidence. . . . We are trying only to loose the intentional
> web which ties them to one another, to rediscover the path of
> the sublimation which preserves and transforms the perceived
> world into the spoken word. . . . The awareness of truth
> advances like a crab, turned toward its point of
> departure. . . such is the living operation that sustains the
> signs of the algorithm.[15]

Here we have his last valiant attempt to turn structuralism into a
branch of dialectical phenomenology and to show its existential
and experiential roots. After writing these words he abandoned the
project altogether, never permitted it to be published, and turned
to his newer, second, and final "dialectical" project, *The Visible
and the Invisible* which on May 3, 1961, he died while writing.

Here (in *The Visible and the Invisible*) the statement of his
method is intransigent, almost defiant.

The dialectic, he writes, is "what we have been looking for."
It is not the dialectic of Hegel, a dialectic of ideas rather than
of being. It is not the dialectic of Sartre which, with its gloomy
and unalleviated negativity, leaves no room for genuine synthesis
but remains caught in a subject-object duality which cannot be
overcome. It is Merleau-Ponty's own dialectic, an "unstable (in
the sense chemists give to the word)" dialectic, unable to form in
theses without denaturing itself. The synthesis is itself the
point of departure rather than the point of arrival. The ambiguous, incarnate, unstable being-in-the-world which is at the
origin of both the visible and the invisible is already both.
Synthesis precedes thesis and antithesis and also succeeds it.

> One of the tasks of the dialectic, as a situational
> thought, a thought in contact with being, is to shake off the
> false evidence, to denounce the significations cut off from
> the experience of being, emptied – and to criticize itself in
> the measure it itself becomes one of them.[16]

The dialectic is not the dialectic of "philosophy" but of
being. "Oh, Dialectic!" he writes, and in words which remind us of
Handel's *Messiah*, apostrophizes:

> . . .the dialectic is almost someone; like the irony of
> things, it is a spell cast over the world that turns our
> expectations into derision, a sly power behind our back that
> confounds us, and, to top it all, has its own [words
> accidentally deleted] it is not only a risk of non-sense,

therefore, but much worse: the assurance that the things have *another sense* than that which we. . . recognize in them.[17]

Of course citing from *The Visible and the Invisible* is a hazardous enterprise. It is not a book. Even in its more finished sections it is really only the incompletely corrected notes for a book. It has many stream-of-thought passages which go on without paragraphs for pages. Merleau-Ponty recognized its unfinished and uncorrected nature, its lack of rigor, its lack of consistency, its lack of elementary clarity. Some pages were apparently written so fast, his ideas just tumbling out in a heated desire to get them all down before they ceased, that even the reader gets the feeling of being driven by an untamed niagara. Some even say that, at this stage, he was no longer getting enough blood to the brain. Therefore our conclusions, in the absence of Merleau-Ponty's own corrections and rewritings, must be tentative.

But one of the fairly well developed uses to which he puts his second, new, and final dialectic was the study of language, since he had to undo or at least reinterpret his earlier excursus into structuralism. When he takes up language in *The Visible and the Invisible*, his style of exposition alone shows that he has completely abandoned structuralism of any kind. He writes:

It is by considering language that we would best see how we are to and how we are not to return to the things themselves. . . . Language is a power of error, since it cuts the continuous tissue that joins us vitally to the thing and to the past and is installed between ourselves and that tissue like a screen. The philosopher speaks, but this is a weakness in him, and an unexplicable weakness: he should keep silent, coincide in silence, and rejoin in Being a philosophy that is there ready-made. But yet everything comes to pass as though he wished to put into words the certain silence he hearkens to within himself. His entire "work" is this absurd effort. . . . One has to believe, then, that language is not simply the contrary of the truth, of coincidence, that there is or could be a language of coincidence. . . . Language is a life, is our life and the life of things. . . . It is the error of the semantic philosophies to close up language as if it spoke only of itself: language lives only from silence. . . thought itself is "structured like language." . . . If we consider the ready-made language, the secondary and empirical operation of translation, of coding and decoding, the artificial languages, the technical relation between a sound and a meaning which are joined only by expressed convention are therefore ideally isolable. . . the problem of language is "only a regional problem." But if, on the contrary, we consider the speaking word, the assuming of the conventions of his native language as something natural by him who lives within that language, the folding over within him of the visible and lived experience of language, and of language upon the visible and lived experience, the exchange between the articulations of his mute language and those of his speech, finally that operative language which has no need to be translated into significations and thoughts, that language-thing which counts as an arm, as action, as offence and as seduction because it brings to the surface all the deep-rooted relations of the lived experience when it takes form, and which is the language of life and action, but also that of literature and poetry – then this logos is an absolute universal theme, it is the theme of philosophy. . . The pre-language of the mute world. . . called forth by the voices of silence.[18]

We end with this long excerpt from his final discussion of language because it encapsulates as succinctly as he ever did, holding contradictories together in an unstable solution, the place of language in his final philosophy of being. The triumph of dialectics is absolute.

NOTES TO INTRODUCTION

1. See the interesting study by Klaus Boer, *Maurice Merleau-Ponty: Die Entwicklung seines Strukturdenkens* (Bonn: Bouvier, 1978).

2. Maurice Merleau-Ponty, *Humanism and Terror*, Tr. John O'Neill, Boston, Beacon Press, 1969, p. 40. See also my book review in *The Journal of Value Inquiry*, Winter, 1970.

3. Ibid., pp. 42-43.

4. Ibid., p. 42.

5. Ibid., p. 48.

6. Ibid., p. 68.

7. Ibid., p. 29.

8. Ibid., p. 59.

9. Ibid., p. 137.

10. Ibid., p. 33.

11. Ibid., p. 21.

12. Ibid., p. 62.

13. Ibid., p. 187.

14. Ibid., pp. xix, 15, 154.

15. Ibid., p. xx.

16. Ibid., p. 153.

17. Ibid., pp. 129-130.

18. Ibid., pp. 15, 113, 119.

19. Ibid., pp. 17-18.

20. Ibid., p. 55.

21. Ibid., pp. 11, 31, 55, 155.

22. Ibid., p. xxxviii.

23. Ibid., p. 11.

24. Ibid., p. 109.

25. Ibid., pp. 143-144.

26. Ibid., pp. 153 ff.

27. Albert Rabil, *Merleau-Ponty, Existentialist of the Social World*, New York, Columbia University Press, 1967. See also my book review in *The Journal of Value Inquiry*, Fall, 1968.

28. Ibid., p. 217.

29. Ibid., pp. 220-221.

30. Ibid., p. 222.

31. Ibid., p. 223.

NOTES FOR CHAPTER ONE

1. Merleau-Ponty made four major attempts to explain Husserl's conception of "rational grammar", and to show that Husserl abandoned, in his later writings, his early proposal for an eidetics of grammar, namely in (1) the section on "*linguistics*" in "Les sciences de l'homme et la phénoménologie" (Cours de Sorbonne, Paris, Centre de Documentation Universitaire, 1951), English translation, "Phenomenology and the Sciences of Man," in *The Primacy of Perception and Other Essays*, ed. James M. Edie, Northwestern University Press, 1964, 78–85, (2) "Sur la phénoménologie du langage", in *Problèmes actuels de la phénoménologie* (Paris, 1952), English translation, "On the Phenomenology of Language", tr. Richard C. McCleary, in *Signs*, Northwestern University Press, 1964, 84–97, (3) "Le philosophe et la sociologie," *Cahiers internationaux de sociologie* (1951); English translation, "The Philosopher and Sociology", in *Signs*, 98–113, and (4) *La prose du monde*, Paris, 1969, 37ff. I consider this attempt on the part of Merleau-Ponty to "push Husserl further than he wanted to go himself" (cf. *The Primacy of Perception*, p. 72, for a similar admission) to be not only historically unsound, given the fact that there is no evidence whatever that Husserl ever abandoned his early views on logical and universal grammatical invariants, but also phenomenologically misguided. See my article, "Can Grammar Be Thought?" in *Patterns of the Life-World, Essays in Honor of John Wild*, Northwestern University Press, 1970, 315–45.

2. Note that Wittgenstein was also quite innocent of scientific linguistics, though in his discovery of the algorithmic structure of the kind of linguistic rules that always "permit us to go on" and thus give language its structured and yet open-ended and innovative potentialities he employed ideas that are fundamental to structuralism insofar as these apply to language. I am indebted to Professor Newton Garver, whose seminar on Wittgenstein I attended, for showing me several of these "structuralist" insights into Wittgenstein's *Philosophical Investigations*.

3. A number of "phenomenologists" have taken up their cudgels, such as Sartre in a special issue of *L'Arc*, Paris, 1966, 87 ff. (where he argues that structuralism misunderstands the ontological dependence of *la langue* on *la parole* and ignores the historicity of language), and Mikel Dufrenne in *Pour l'homme*, Paris, 1968, which is a critical analysis of each of the several versions of structuralism currently in vogue in France. Paul Ricoeur has also criticized structuralism in the manner one would expect from a phenomenologist and a philosopher of the *cogito*, first in a special issue of *Esprit* dedicated to this debate,

"Structure et hermeneutique", *Esprit* (1963), 593-653, and then in a more definitive article, "La structure, le mot, l'evenement", *Esprit* (1967), 801-21, but in his most recent work he has attempted, more and more, to accommodate himself to the Structuralists, and particularly to Claude Levi-Strauss. These remarks are now in 1986 somewhat, perforce, dated, though my own heart remains with the Structuralists and the hope they still show for a methodological renewal in the human sciences. But, by now, it is the post-structuralists, especially the deconstructionists who have gained the shifting affections of the avant-garde but deconstructionism can barely lay claim to the territory of the sociology of knowledge and certainly not philosophy. For a very general overview, one might want to consult Stephen H. Watson, "Merleau-Ponty's Involvement with Saussure," in *Continental Philosophy in America*, edd., Hugh Silverman, John Sallis, and Thomas Seebohm, Pittsburgh, Pa: Duquesne University Press, 1983.

4. This is particularly true of Lacan and Lévi-Strauss, but is also true of Derrida and others.

5. *Phénoménologie de la perception* (Paris, 1945), English translation, *Phenomenology of Perception*, by Colin Smith (New York and London, 1962), p. 188. I will note here, for the record, that though the quotations from Merleau-Ponty in this article are taken from the English translations as a matter of principle, I have occasionally slightly corrected these translations when this was found necessary to give the exact nuance of the original French.

6. *Ibid.*, 183, 186, 193-94.

7. *Ibid.*, 184, 189.

8. *Cours de l'Université de Lyon (1948)*, unpublished.

9. *Bulletin de psychologie* III (1949), republished in *Bulletin de psychologie* XVIII (1964), 226-59. English translation by Hugh J. Silverman, *Consciousness and the Acquisition of Language*, with a "Foreword" by James M. Edie (Northwestern University Press, 1973).

10. *Cours de Sorbonne* (Paris, Centre de Documentation Universitaire, 1951), English translation, "Phenomenology and the Sciences of Man", *The Primacy of Perception and Other Essays*, ed. by James M. Edie (Northwestern University Press, 1964), 43-95.

11. An address read in Brusseles on April 13, 1951, in *Problèmes actuels de la phénoménologie* (Paris, 1952), reprinted in *Signes* (Paris, 1960). English translation by Richard C. McCleary, "On the Phenomenology of Language", *Signs* (Northwestern University Press, 1964), 84-97.

12. *Cahiers internationaux de sociologie* (1951), in *Signs*, "The Philosopher and Sociology", 98-113.

13. *Les Temps Modernes* (June–July, 1952), in *Signs*, "Indirect Language and the Voices of Silence", 39–83.

14. *Revue de metaphysique et de morale* (1962), 401–09. English translation in *The Primacy of Perception*, "An Unpublished Text by Maurice Merleau-Ponty: A Prospectus of His Work", 3–11. This is a document Merleau-Ponty prepared when he was a candidate for the chair of philosophy at the Collège de France in 1953. It gives a historical outline of the development of his thought and shows how he himself interpreted his growing interest in language, and the place of his philosophy of language in his work as a whole.

15. (Paris, 1953). English translation, *In Praise of Philo-sophy*, by John Wild and James M. Edie (Northwestern University Press, 1963). In this book, which is his inaugural address at the Collège de France, Merleau-Ponty interprets the thought of all his "predecessors" and those to whose thought he is particularly indebted. It is here for the first time that he credits Saussure and structural linguistics with developing a "theory of signs" (pp. 54–55) that could serve as a better basis for a philosophy of history than the thought of either Marx or Hegel. This is a theme to which he frequently returns in his later writings, such as in *La prose du monde* (Paris, 1969), pp. 33ff.: "*Saussure a l'immense mérite d'accomplir la démarche qui libère l'histoire de l'histori-cisme et rend possible une nouvelle conception de la raison. Si chaque mot, chaque forme d'une langue, pris séparément, recoive au cours de son histoire une serie de significations discordantes, il n'y a pas d'équivoque dans la langue totale considerée en chacun de ses moments. Les mutations de chaque appareil signifiant, si inattendues qu'elles paraissent à le considerer tout seul, sont solidaires de celles de tous les autres et cela fait que l'en-semble reste moyen d'une communication.*" Whether Saussure really *deserves* (or would himself have accepted) the role Merleau-Ponty assigns him is, of course, another matter. At least one commenta-tor, in an article criticizing Merleau-Ponty's over-optimistic interpretation of Saussure, doubts this. Cf. Maurice Lagueux, "Merleau-Ponty et la linguistique de Saussure", *Dialogue* (1965), 351–64.

16. *Résumés de cours, Collège de France, 1952–1960* (Paris, 1968). English translation, *Themes from the Lectures of the Collège de France 1952–1960*, by John O'Neill (Northwestern Univer-sity Press, 1970), 3–11.

17. *Ibid.*, 12–18.

18. *Ibid.*, 19–26.

19. *La Nouvelle Revue Francaise* (Octobre, 1959), in *Signs*, "From Mauss to Claude Lévi-Strauss", 114–25.

20. *La prose du monde*, ed. by Claude Lefort (Paris, 1969). English translation by John O'Neill (Northwestern University Press, 1973).

21. *Le visible et l'invisible*, ed. by Claude Lefort (Paris, 1964). Translation by Alphonso Lingis (Northwestern University Press, 1968).

22. In an interesting article we mentioned in note 15, Maurice Lagueux accuses Merleau-Ponty of misrepresenting Saussure on at least two points, namely by claiming falsely that Saussure gave the primacy to *la parole* over *la langue* in his study of language and, further, by stating in his article "On the Phenomenology of Language" that Saussure distinguished "a synchronic linguistics of speech" from "a diachronic linguistics of language" (see *Signs*, 86). The fact is, as Lagueux shows, that both *synchrony* and *diachrony* are aspects of *la langue*, whereas the study of *la parole* falls completely outside a scientific study of language. While it is difficult not to accept Lagueux's verdict, it is nevertheless true that many of Saussure's own texts are ambiguous and the account Merleau-Ponty gives in *La prose du monde* (pp. 33 ff.), for instance, would meet most if not all of Lagueux's criticisms and would give us solid ground for holding that even though Merleau-Ponty sometimes, even frequently, quotes Saussure very freely, he does not seriously misunderstand his intent. The essential point is that one must distinguish a science of the given state of a linguistic system (*la langue*), which Saussure calls "synchronic linguistics", from the historical science of the linguistic changes that any given language has undergone, which Saussure calls "diachronic linguistics". Now clearly the object with which diachronic linguistics deals is something that can *only* be studied "objectively" and in which present, ongoing human experience can play no essential role. But conversely, the object of synchronic linguistics, though it is the "form" or "system" of the present state of a given language and not the speech act itself, is nevertheless nothing other than the presently given, incubating and changing structure of the sum total of all presently recognized acts of speaking that take place within a given community, and it is nothing but the description of the structure of these acts. Moreover, since each historical state that can be distinguished in the diachronic study of a given language was at one time a living, future-directed, synchronic system, we can see the sense in which "a synchronic linguistics of speech" envelops and takes precedence over "a diachronic linguistics of language". Once one fully understands why Merleau-Ponty speaks this way and what he means by the terms one will see that he is not opposed to Saussure in any essential respect.

23. Ferdinand de Saussure, *Cours de linguistique générale* (Paris, 1922), pp. 30, 36-39. It is interesting to note that, until most recently, the analytical philosophy of language, as it developed from Moore and Russell, through Wittgenstein, and as it has lately culminated in "Oxford philosophy", takes just the opposite approach. There, it is the "speech act" that is the central focus of attention and very few of the important philosophers in this group have shown any special interest in linguistic structuralism or, indeed, in scientific linguistics at all until very recently. Merleau-Ponty is apparently the first philosopher of any great influence to have attempted an assessment of the importance of linguistics for the philosophy of language, but it is noteworthy that he also gives the primacy to *la parole* or the speech act.

24. *Signs*, 117.

25. *Signs*, 39.

26. *Themes from the Lectures at the Collège de France*, 19-20. The thesis that the "meaning" of words is as much in the interstices between them, in what is *not said*, in the silence that surrounds speech, is one that Merleau-Ponty develops primarily in his later writings and above all in *The Visible and the Invisible*. This is particularly important for a theory of literature.

27. Ferdinand de Saussure, *Cours*, p. 99. Lagueux points out, on p. 356 of the article cited in note 15, that Merleau-Ponty sometimes writes as if Saussure himself had questioned the arbitrary and conventional character of the relationship between the "acoustic image" (*signifiant*) and its associated "concept" (*signifie*), and it is therefore necessary to point out that it is not Saussure, but Merleau-Ponty who gives this interpretation to his notion of the "signs". Nevertheless, it seems clear that Saussure did indeed think of the "sign" as containing indissolubly, the two aspects of sound *and* meaning. In a passage that Lagueux does not cite (*Cours*, p. 145), Saussure writes that the "bilateral unity" of the physical aspect and the meaning aspect of word-signs should not be compared "to the unity of the human person, composed of body and soul", conceived of as two separate substances joined in a union in which each maintains its distinctive characteristics and independence the one from the other, but rather on the analogy of something like a "chemical compound" in which the components lose their distinctive identities when joined (taken separately, as we know, hydrogen and oxygen have none of the properties of water but, when joined, they result in a *tertium quid* that is neither the one nor the other but has the new properties that emerge from their union). Whatever one may think of this wild "chemical" analogy, it is clear that Saussure's

theory of the sign does call into question, if not the distinction, at least the separation, of the *signifiant* from the
signifié within the sign.

28. *Phenomenology of Perception*, pp. 187-88. Lest one be
tempted to think that Merleau-Ponty may perhaps have disowned or
mitigated his ideas on this score in his later writings, it is
useful to cite a passage from his last work, *La prose du monde*, p.
161: "*Nous avons plusieurs fois contesté que le langage ne fut lié
à ce qu'il signifie que par l'habitude et la convention; il en est
beaucoup plus proche et beaucoup plus eloigné. En un sens il
tourne le dos a la signification, il ne s'en soucie pas. . . . Les
phonologues ont admirablement vu cette vie sublinguistique dont
toute l'industrie est de différéncier et de mettre en système des
signes, et cela n'est pas vrai seulement des phonèmes avant les
mots, c'est vrai aussi des mots et de toute la langue, qui n'est
pas d'abord signe de certains significations, mais pouvoir reglé
de differencier la chaine verbale selon des dimensions caracteris-
tiques de chaque langue. En un sens, le langage n'a jamais affaire
qu'à lui-meme: dans le monologue interieur comme dans le dialogue
il n'y a pas de "pensées": ce sont des paroles que les paroles
suscitent et, dans la mesure même ou nous "pensons" plus pleine-
ment, les paroles remplissent si exactement notre esprit qu'elles
n'y laissent pas un coin vide pour des pensées pures et pour des
significations qui ne solent pas langagières."*

29. Alphonse De Waelhens, *Une philosophie de l'ambiguité:
L'existentialisme de Maurice Merleau-Ponty* (Louvain, 1951),
p. 159.

30. *Phenomenology of Perception*, p.189.

31. *Phenomenology. . . .*, p. 179.

32. *Phenomenology*, p. 179.

33. *La prose du monde*, pp. 45, 161.

34. Ferdinand de Saussure, *Cours*, p. 166.

35. Cf. "La conscience et l'acquisition du langage", *Bulletin
de Psychologie*, 226-59, esp. 255ff.; *Signs*, 91; *Themes from the
Lectures at the Collège de France*, 13-15; *The Visible and the
Invisible*, pp. 124-25; *La prose du monde*, pp. 13-15.

36. Cf. Alphonse De Waelhens, "La philosophie du langage
selon M. Merleau-Ponty", in *Existence of Signification* (Louvain,
1958), 135.

37. Each word "*has* a meaning only in so far as it is sus-
tained in this meaning-function by all the others. . . . For a
word to keep its sense it has to be held in place by all the
others". ("La conscience et l'acquisition du langage", 256).

38. See note 22.

39. Noam Chomsky, *Language and Mind* (New York, 1968), p. 17.

40. See my article, "Can Grammar Be Thought?" 340-41.

41. *La prose du monde*, pp. 37ff., 166ff.

42. See my article, "Husserl's Conception of *The Grammatical* and Contemporary Linguistics", in a volume entitled *Life-World and Consciousness, Essays in Honor of Aron Gurwitsch*, ed. by Lester E. Embree, Northwestern University Press, 1972, 233-261.

43. *Signs*, 87.

44. *Signs*, 87.

45. *Phenomenology of Perception*, p. 188.

46. *Signs*, 119.

47. *Phenomenology. . .*, p. 189.

48. *Signs*, 87.

49. *La prose du monde*, p. 56.

50. *La prose du monde*, p. 56.

51. *Signs*, 118-20, emphasis mine.

52. *The Visible and the Invisible*, p. 116.

53. *Signs*, 119.

54. *The Visible. . .*, p. 116. Cf. *The Primacy of Perception and Other Essays*, p. 68.

55. *The Primacy. . .*, p. 70.

56. *Signs*, 105, 107, 109-10, emphasis mine.

57. *The Primacy . . .*, p. 53. It would be interesting to compare the phenomenological method of eidetic intuition (*Wesenschau*), which falls somewhere between an aprioristic method of deduction and a pure empiricism of induction, with C. S. Peirce's theory of *abduction*. Peirce also saw clearly that creative scientific thinking is not a matter of pure induction but involves some kind of rational intuition into the facts that is provided not by the facts themselves but by the "guessing instinct" of the subject, which enables him "to put a limit on admissible hypotheses" and to construct a general law that will cover all the facts of a certain category on the basis of a very small number of instances, and even frequently on the basis of a single instance. See C. S. Peirce, "The Logic of Abduction", in *Peirce's Essays in the Philosophy of Science*, ed. Vincent Tomas (New York, 1957). It is interesting that Noam Chomsky (*Language and Mind*, pp. 78 ff), who is unacquainted with phenomenology in any of its forms but who feels the need to discover the method by which a child, for instance, learns a language on the basis of a "knowledge" that extends, from the beginning stages, enormously beyond his actual experience and even enables him to recognize much of the data of his actual experience as defective and deviant, suggests that a theory of abduction might serve this purpose.

1. This is the primary problem, but one might point out: not just for Merleau-Ponty. It is a problem for William James who must explain just *why* the world "plays into the hands of logic." It is a problem for Husserl who must explain how perception (*Erfahrung*) founds judgment (*Urteil*). At least the phenomenologists know where the problem is; the logical positivists go on blithely accepting both the reduction to sense data and all the laws of formal logic without any theory of how they do or can fit together.

2. In the essay entitled "The Primacy of Perception and its Philosophical Consequences," which was a presentation of the central argument of the *Phenomenology of Perception* to the Société francaise de philosophie, November 23, 1946. See *The Primacy of Perception*, ed. James M. Edie (Evanston, Ill.: Northwestern University Press, 1964), pp. 12 ff.

3. "An Unpublished Text by Maurice Merleau-Ponty: A Prospectus of His Work," in *Primacy of Perception*, p. 11. This is the English translation of the program which Merleau-Ponty submitted to the professors of the Collège de France in presenting his candidacy for a chair of philosophy in 1952.

4. See the "Avertissement" by Claude Lefort to Merleau-Ponty, *La Prose du monde* (Paris, 1969), pp. i, ix–xi.

5. *Primacy of Perception*, p. 20.

6. *Ibid.*, p. 19.

7. *Ibid.*, p. 20.

8. *Ibid.*, p. 22.

9. *Ibid.*, p. 17.

10. *Phenomenology of Perception*, tr. Colin Smith (New York: Humanities Press, 1962), pp. 414–439.

11. *Primacy of Perception*, p. 215.

12. *Phenomenology of Perception*, p. 394; italics mine.

13. "An Unpublished Text. . ." in *Primacy of Perception*, p. 6.

14. *Primacy of Perception*, p. 17.

15. "An Unpublished Text. . ." in *Primacy of Perception*, p. 6.

16. *Ibid.*, p. 10.

17. *Ibid*; italics mine.

18. *La Prose de monde*, p. 56. Also see my article, "Was Merleau-Ponty a Structuralist?" *Semiotica* IV (1971), 315 ff. and Chapter I above, pp. 31–32.

19. F. P. Ramsey, *The Foundations of Mathematics*, pp. 115–116, as quoted by Renford Bambrough in "Universals and Family

Resemblances," in *Wittgenstein*, ed. George Pitcher (Garden City, N.Y.: Anchor Books, 1966), p. 198. I am indebted to Margaret Urban Coyne for first pointing out Ramsey's maxim to me; I had earlier described Merleau-Ponty's method in the *Phenomenology of Perception* in just this way; see *Semiotica*, IV, 299ff.

20. *Primacy of Perception*, p. 20; *Phenomenology of Perception*, p. 386.

21. *Phenomenology of Perception*, p. 396.

22. *Ibid.*, p. 385.

23. *Ibid.*, pp. 385, 386, 388; italics mine.

24. *Phenomenology of Perception*, p. 394.

25. *Ibid.*, p. 377.

26. I am using this term in a very vague sense here. I am not taking sides for or against Kant, who would say that the apriori is what consciousness has put into things, or for or against a philosopher of language like Garver, who would say that the apriori is a "grammatical" matter. (See Newton Garver, "Analyticity and Grammar," *The Monist*, 51 [1967], 397 ff.) I am very sympathetic to the latter approach so long as by "grammar" one understands the whole of linguistic usage, and with the proviso that the relation of thinking to using language be understood in the manner in which Husserl understands it in *Formal and Transcendental Logic*. This is obviously not the place to go into these difficult problems. I am using "linguistic" in this context as a synonym for "thought."

27. See Chapter I above, pp. 24–44.

28. Particularly in "On the Phenomenology of Language" (1951), in *Signs*, tr. Richard C. McCleary (Evanston, Ill.: Northwestern University Press, 1964), pp. 84–97; in "Indirect Language and the Voices of Silence" (1951), in *Signs*, pp. 39–83; in the completed sections of *La Prose du monde*; and in several of his courses at the Collège de France (the outlines of which are published in *Themes from the Lectures at the Collège de France, 1952-1960*, tr. John O'Neill [Evanston, Ill.: Northwestern University Press, 1970]). For a complete bibliography of Merleau-Ponty's writings on language in his "middle period" see Chapter I above, pp. 18–19.

29. These are the "final pages" we have; they were not the end he himself planned for this uncompleted book.

30. *The Visible and the Invisible*, ed. Claude Lefort, tr. Alphonso Lingis (Evanston, Ill.: Northwestern University Press, 1968), p. 132; italics mine.

31. The thesis mentioned here is dealt with somewhat more fully in my paper on "The Present Status of the Phenomenology of Language," which was read at the Fifth Lexington Conference on

Pure and Applied Phenomenology, "Language and Language Distur-
bances," Lexington, Kentucky, April 13-15, 1972. Published as
Language and Language Disturbances, ed. Erwin W. Strauss (Duquesne
University Press, 1974).

NOTES TO CHAPTER THREE

1. The most recent, authoritative and complete discussion of this literature is in: Klaus Boer, *Maurice Merleau-Ponty - Die Entwicklung seines Strukturdenkens* (Bonn: Bouvier) 1978. Boer gives an almost complete bibliography with interpretative discussion of a high order. Though I disagree with his central thesis - which is opposed in what I write below - his discussion is to be highly recommended. I intend to devote a subsequent article to a more minute examination of his own viewpoint. In this study I am treating the general current tendency, of which he is the best example, in Merleau-Ponty studies.

2. I have dealt with this more fully in: James M. Edie, *Speaking and Meaning*, Indiana Univeristy Press, 1976, Chapter III.

3. James M. Edie, "Foreword," Maurice Merleau-Ponty, *Consciousness and the Acquisition of Language*, tr. Hugh J. Silverman, Northwestern University Press, 1973, pp. xix-xx.

4. Claude Lefort, "Editor's Preface," Maurice Merleau-Ponty, *The Prose of the World*, tr. John O'Neill, Northwestern University Press, 1973, pp. xv ff.

5. Maurice Merleau-Ponty, *Signs*, tr. Richard C. McCleary, Northwestern University Press, 1964, p. 117.

6. Maurice Merleau-Ponty, *Themes from the Lectures at the Collège de France*, tr. John O'Neill, Northwestern University Press, 1970, pp. 19-20.

7. See "Foreword," *Consciousness and the Acquisition of Language, op. cit.*, pp. xxvii-xxix.

8. *Consciousness and the Acquisition of Language, op. cit.*, p. 93.

9. *Ibid.*, p. 97.

10. *Ibid.*, p. 99.

11. *Ibid.*, p. 93.

12. Maurice Merleau-Ponty, "Phenomenology and the Sciences of Man," *The Primacy of Perception*, ed. James M. Edie, Northwestern University Press, 1964, pp. 81-82.

13. *Ibid.*, p. 81.

14. Ibid.

15. *Ibid.*, p. 84.

16. Maurice Merleau-Ponty, *In Praise of Philosophy*, tr. James M. Edie and John Wild, Northwestern University Press, 1963, p. 56, emphasis mine.

17. *Ibid.*, pp. 54-55.

18. James M. Edie, "Phenomenology in the United States (1974)," *Journal of the British Society for Phenomenology*, 1974, pp. 206 ff. In this article I think I demonstrate the importance

of Gurwitsch for Merleau-Ponty and provide the essential, though perhaps not the exhaustive, bibliographical information relevant to their collaboration in the years 1933-1940. The article by Gurwitsch, "Quelques aspects et quelques développements de la psychologie de la forme," *Journal de psychologie normale et pathologique*, 1936, pp. 413-470, was one on which Merleau-Ponty is cited as a collaborator; it is also one which provided the French philosophical world of that time with the most extensive bibliography on Gestalt theory which had been published up to that time. This bibliography is very similar to that in Merleau-Ponty's *Structure of Behavior*. See also Merleau-Ponty's Examination of Gestalt Psychology, *Research in Phenomenology*, Vol. X (1980) and, id., "Gurwitsch's Critique of Merleau-Ponty," *Journal of the British Society for Phenomenology*, Vol. XII (1981).

19. *Consciousness and the Acquisition of Language, op. cit.*, p. 100.

20. Raymond Boudon, *A quoi sert la notion de "structure"?* Paris, 1968, p. 42, and *passim*. In this connection a slight addition is in order. From the point of view of the history of ideas in general Aron Gurwitsch occupies a focal place as the one person who did more than any other to introduce first, French,and then American, philosophers to the writings of the Gestalt psychologists and all the work that had been accomplished in German psychology beginning with E. Rubin's *Visuell wahrgenommene Figuren* in 1921, through the work of Lewin, Metzgar, Koffka, Koehler, Gelb and Goldstein, and the other major Gestalt psychologists, through the period he stayed in Paris (1933-1940), and, thereafter, in America, right up to the time of his death. His period in Paris was a most productive one and among the papers he published in that time in various French journals several were specifically on Gestalt psychology and its philosophical importance. [The most important of these are the following: (1) "La Place de la psychologie dans l'ensemble des sciences," *Revue de synthése*, VIII, 1934, pp. 169-185, (2) "Psychologie du langage," *Revue Philosophique de la France et de l'Etranger* CXX, 1935, pp. 399-439, (3) "Quelques aspects et quelques développements de la psychologie de la forme," *Journal de psychologie normale et pathologique*, XXXIII, 1936, pp. 413-470, (4) "Développement historique de la Gestalt psychologie," *Thales* II, 1935, pp. 167-176, (5) "Le fonctionnement de l'organisme d'apres K. Goldstein," *Journal de psychologie normale et pathologique*, XXXVI, 1939, pp. 107-138, (6) "La science biologique d'apres K. Goldstein," *Révue philosophique de la France et de l'Etranger*, CXXIX, 1940, pp. 244-265. The results of all these studies, together with other work, are included in *The Field of Consciousness*. These essays are translated in Aron Gurwitsch,

Studies in Phenomenology and Psychology (Northwestern University Press, 1966).

This presentation of the work of German psychologists to the French learned world was the more fateful and influential in that during this period Gurwitsch came to know the young Merleau-Ponty, the man who was to become "the greatest of the French phenomenologists" (in the words of Paul Ricoeur). Merleau-Ponty had begun to become interested in Gestalt psychology shortly after passing his *Aggregation en philosophie* in 1930 and had even read Gurwitsch's doctoral dissertation, *Phanomenologie der Thematik und des reinen Ich*, before he actually met Gurwitsch. [See Lester E. Embree, "Biographical Sketch of Aron Gurwitsch," in *Life-World and Consciousness, op. cit.*, p. xxiv.] He had also heard of Husserl and Heidegger by then and had attended (though he hardly understood German) the four lectures Edmund Husserl gave at the Sorbonne on "The Introduction to Transcendental Phenomenology" in 1929. [Theodore F. Geraets, *Vers une nouvelle philosophie transcendentale, La génèse de la philosophie de Maurice Merleau-Ponty*, The Hague, 1971, p. 7.] But it was only under Gurwitsch in 1933 that he began a systematic study of both phenomenology and Gestalt psychology, work that was greatly reinforced by the influence of his friend Sartre after the latter's return from a year of study in Germany in 1935. It turned out that during the 1933-1934 term Merleau-Ponty, who was then teaching philosophy at a lycée in Beauvais, received a government grant from the Caisse nationale des Sciences to work on his doctoral dissertation in Paris for a year. This was the same year that Gurwitsch arrived in Paris and became attached to the Institut d'Histoire des Sciences [in *The Field of Consciousness* Gurwitsch states that, when he first arrived in Paris from Germany, he was helped by the following institutions: Comité pour les savants etrangers, Comité d'accueil et d'organisation de travail pour les savants étrangers résidants en France, and especially by the Caisse nationale de la Récherche scientifique.] where he gave a series of conferences in 1933-1934 on "Le développement historique de la *Gestalt psychologie*". This course was published in modified form in the *Journal de psychologie normale et pathologique* in 1936 under the title: "Quelques aspects et quelques dévéloppements de la psychologie de la forme". [*Journal de psychologie normale et pathologique*, XXXIII, 1936, pp. 413-470.] At the beginning of this article Gurwitsch thanks Merleau-Ponty for having read it prior to publication (and no doubt helped polish the French). He also thanks Merleau-Ponty in similar fashion at the beginning of another article, namely "Psychologie du langage," *Revue philosophique de la France et de l'Etranger*, CXX, 1935, pp. 399-439. It is clear, therefore, that

Merleau-Ponty had close knowledge of these two texts (and probably of everything else Gurwitsch had written up till then) and may even have collaborated on them to a certain extent. Nevertheless, this fact has been so well forgotten that of all the bibliographies which have been published on Merleau-Ponty, only the two most recent (namely the bibliography assembled by Alexandre Métraux for Xavier Tilliette's *Merleau-Ponty ou la mesure de l'homme*, Paris, 1970, p. 174, and that to be found in Theodore F. Geraets, *Vers une nouvelle philosophie transcendentale, op. cit.*, p. 210) mention the first whereas not even these two most complete and careful bibliographies even mention "Psychologie du langage," an article which reviews the contributions of Gestalt (and other) psychologists to the study of language and whose echo is to be found in Merleau-Ponty's first courses on language, namely his course on "Langage et communication" at Lyon in 1947-1948, and in "Conscience et l'aquisition du langage," at the Sorbonne in 1949-50 (always without any mention of Gurwitsch). This raises the question of the strange reticence on the part of Merleau-Ponty towards Gurwitsch. We know that he followed Gurwitsch's course at the Institut d'Histoire des Sciences et des Techniques de l'Universite de Paris in 1933-1934, we know that Gurwitsch gave Merleau-Ponty unpublished material on Goldstein's work on Schneider (see Embree, *op. cit.*, p. xxiv), and that it was Gurwitsch who first gave Merleau-Ponty knowledge of the work of Alfred Schutz. But, strangely, there is no mention of Gurwitsch at all in Merleau-Ponty's *Structure of Behavior* even though he is dealing with material very similar to Gurwitsch's and using a bibliography very much like that to be found at the end of "Quelques aspects et quelques developpements de la pschologie de la forme." In *Phenomenology of Perception* Gurwitsch occurs only in the bibliography, where this article (but without mention of his own collaboration) and Gurwitsch's review of Husserl's *Nachwort zu meinen Ideen* are listed. It is no doubt this complete silence on Merleau-Ponty's part which misled Geraets into making the rather fatuous remark that thanks to Merleau-Ponty's study of Koffka, Koehler, Goldstein, et al. he was able when the occasion arose, to help Gurwitsch write his article on "Quelques aspects et quelques developpements de la psychologie de la forme" (*op. cit.*, p. 13) whereas it was in actuality the other way around. It was largely because of Gurwitsch that Merleau-Ponty was able to make such rapid and seemingly effortless progress in his systematic study of these and other Gestalt psychologies. It is true that Merleau-Ponty *could* have known of Gestalt psychology through the work of the French psychologist Paul Guillaume, whose first important article in French, "La theorie de la forme" was published in 1925 (in *Journal de psychologie*). But it is also quite possible that it was from Gurwitsch himself (who cites this article in "Quelques aspects. . ." together with the other papers which Guillaume had published up to that time in the German journal *Psychologische Forschung*) that Merleau-Ponty first came to Guillaume. In any case, in 1933, Gurwitsch already knew more of Guillaume's work than Merleau-Ponty could have learned from what there was of Guillaume's work available to him in French (Guillaume's first major book did not appear until 1936). Moreover the bibliography which Gurwitsch provided as an appendix to his article "Quelques aspects. . ." is certainly the most extensive bibliography on Gestalt psychology to have been published in any French journal up to that time, and most all of the items listed in it are used heavily by Merleau-Ponty in his later works. Thus the reality of Gurwitsch's influence is undeniable. Merleau-Ponty's silence about this influence is mysterious and has led such commentators as Geraets into historical errors.

Thus, both through his own numerous publications on Gestalt psychology in French and possibly even more importantly though indirectly, through the later influence of Merleau-Ponty, Gurwitsch served as a conduit for the transmission of this important body of knowledge to French philosophy. [Gurwitsch also had considerable influence on Sartre, but this was more through Merleau-Ponty than directly (see Embree, *op. cit.*, p. xxiv.)]

21. James M. Edie, *Speaking and Meaning, op. cit.*, pp. 175 ff.

22. Maurice Merleau-Ponty, *Sense and Non-Sense*, tr. Dreyfus, Northwestern University Press, 1964, p. 63.

23. Maurice Merleau-Ponty, "An Unpublished Text," *Primacy of Perception, op. cit.*, pp. 3–11. this "Prospectus" of Merleau-Ponty's work, written by himself, and carefully interpreted by Claude Lefort in the "Editor's Preface" to *The Prose of the World*, was Merleau-Ponty's own assessment of his past achievements and his plans for future work at the time he presented himself as a candidate for a chair at the Collège de France.

24. The principal flaw of a recent study (Samuel B. Mallin, *Merleau-Ponty's Philosophy*, Yale University Press, 1979) is that it bases itself on "Merleau-Ponty's full-length works, the *Phenomenology of Perception* and *The Visible and the Invisible*" (p. 4). Whatever the justification for leaving out Merleau-Ponty's other books, there is no justification *at all* for treating *The Visible and the Invisible* as a completed work in any sense. As a work of interpretation this book (by Mullin) attempts to explain *the clear* by the obscure.

25. This point has been made very cogently, with complete historical documentation, by George L. Kline, "The Existential Rediscovery of Hegel and Marx," *Phenomenology and Existentialism*, eds. Lee and Mandelbaum, John Hopkins University Press, 1967, pp. 113 ff.

26. Though the opposite principle of interpretation, in the case of Merleau-Ponty, might bear fruit. He himself always interpreted his newest ideas in terms of earlier periods. Thus he re-interprets this dialectical interpretation of phenomenology in terms of Gestalt theory, and his structuralism in terms of both Gestaltism and dialectics. He could not, of course, interpret his unfinished last work in terms of the earlier except in the most incohate manner since he died before completing it. But perhaps his commentators should ponder his own attitude towards his development rather than imposing the criterion: the last is best.

27. Here, in full justice to Merleau-Ponty, it is necessary to remark that he never fell into the excesses of *Derridian* post-structuralism (or deconstructionism) which holds that all "texts" are self-referential. Thus the "post-structuralism" (if I can call it that for want of a better term) of *The Visible and the Invisible* is an entirely different matter from what the Derridians have come to. With his fine sensitivity to the complexities of language in its relation to experience Merleau-Ponty writes, thus, in a typical passage: "It is the error the semantic philosophies to close up language as if it spoke only of itself: *language lives only from silence*, everything we cast to the others has germinated in this great mute land which we never leave. But, because he has experienced within himself the need to speak. . . the Philosopher knows better than anyone. . . that the vision itself, the thought itself, etc. as has been said [by Lacan] is 'structured like language'." *The Visible and the Invisible*, p. 126, emphasis mine. There is a "post-structuralism" about Merleau-Ponty's final thought, but it needs to be given a nuanced interpretation which would eschew equating it with what otherwise goes by that name. I would here like to express my debt to Professor Dorothy Leland who read her comments and critical remarks on this paper at the meeting of the American Philosophical Association in San Francisco in March, 1980. I have greatly profited from her suggestions, on this and other points.

28. *The Visible and the Invisible*, *op. cit.*, p. 65.

29. See, for instance, the papers in *Deconstruction and Criticism*, Bloom, de Man, Derrida, Hartman, Miller, New York, 1979 *passim*. Since most of the persons who treat of dialectical logic in this manner are not, strictly speaking, philosophers but literary critics, and since they write with a special hermetic

style better understood by baptized initiates than those who argue
openly in the forum, it is not always clear exactly what they are
affirming with respect to deconstructionist methodology. It was,
therefore, a great pleasure for the present author to be able to
ask, at the recent meeting of the International Association for
Philosophy and Literature, held in Orono, Maine, in May, 1980, two
"deconstructionists," namely professors Michael Murray and
Rodolphe Gasche, at separate meetings, the question of whether or
not their conception of dialetics and their conception of their
method required the renunciation of the principles of non-contradiction and of identity as these are defined and understood in
formal logic. Both men answered with straightforward, honest, one-
word responses: "Yes."

30. *The Visible and the Invisible, op. cit.*, p. 142.

31. *Ibid.*, p. 123.

32. Albert Rabil, *Merleau-Ponty, Existentialist of the Social World*, Columbia University Press, 1967, pp. 144 ff.

33. *The Prose of the World, op. cit.*, pp. 38 ff, and Edie, *Speaking and Meaning, op. cit.*, pp. 112 ff.

34. Cf. the forthcoming study by Errol Harris, *Formal and Dialectical Logic.* Harris gives careful, detailed, rigorous atten-
tion first, to the metaphysical presuppositions of formal logic *as such*, then to the transcendental presuppositions of formal logic, and, finally, to the "formal" presuppositions of dialectial logic.

NOTES FOR CHAPTER FOUR

1. This presentation to the College de France, entitled "An Unpublished Text," is published in English in *The Primacy of Perception*, ed. James M. Edie, Northwestern University Press, 1964, pp. 3-11.

2. *La Prose du Monde*, ed. Claude Lefort, Paris, 1969. Lefort's preface contains a most valuable account of the vicissitudes of this book from its inception to its abandonment.

3. The important thing to understand in Merleau-Ponty's first concept of structuralism is that it is gestaltist, but gestaltism philosophically interpreted. I have recounted Merleau-Ponty's dependence on Gurwitsch at this early period of his career in: "Phenomenology in the United States (1974)," *Journal of the British Society for Phenomenology*, 1974, pp. 206 ff, and in Chapter III, above.

4. I have identified this position in the list of his several linguistic essays in my introduction to *Consciousness and the Acquisition of Language*, tr. Hugh J. Silverman, Northwestern University Press, 1973, pp. xix ff.

5. *Humanism and Terror*, tr. John O'Neill, Boston, 1969, p. 153.

6. *In Praise of Philosophy*, tr. James M. Edie and John Wild, Northwestern University Press, 1963, p. 55.

7. *The Primacy of Perception, op. cit.*, p. 6.

8. *Ibid.*, p. 8.

9. *Ibid.*, p. 10.

10. *Ibid.*

11. This is the central philosophical argument in *Consciousness and the Acquisition of Language*, and also crops up from time to time in the working notes for *The Visible and the Invisible*.

12. Published in English in *Signs*, tr. Richard C. McCleary, Northwestern University Press, 1964, pp. 84 ff.

13. *The Primacy of Perception, op. cit.*, p. 72.

14. *La Prose du Monde, op. cit.*, p. 56, *The Prose of the World*, tr. John O'Neill, Northwestern University Press, 1973, p. 39.

15. *The Prose of the World, op. cit.*, pp. 121 ff.

16. *The Visible and the Invisible, op. cit.*, p. 92. I am indebted to Martin C. Dillon for helping me understand this obscure passage. I also wish to thank Sonia Kruks for letting me see her book on Merleau-Ponty's political philosophy and for her article "Merleau-Ponty, Hegel and the Dialectic," *Journal of the British Society for Phenomenology*, 1976, pp. 96 ff. Her admirable treatment of Merleau-Ponty's relation to Hegel and her discussion

of how his dialectic differs from Hegel's seems to me definitive. Though her work on this subject is much more extensive than mine, I am happy to see that it does not *essentially* differ from mine. I also find myself in agreement with her analysis and assessment of Merleau-Ponty's two major political works, namely *Humanism and Terror* and *The Adventures of the Dialectic*. It is intriguing that Merleau-Ponty's theoretical crisis over structural linguistics and his political "crisis" were more or less simultaneous, though, up to now, I see no intrinsic connection between them.

17. *Ibid.*, pp. 93-94. In my article on "The Meaning and the Development of Merleau-Ponty's Concept of Structure," *Research in Phenomenology*, Volume X, 1980, pp. 54-55 (cf. Chapter III above), I give a preliminary analysis of how the dialectic of "the visible and the invisible" applies to the entire re-reading of his philosophy. The oppositions can be tentatively and briefly enumerated as follows:

1) The perception of objects which are not, strictly speaking, given to me in perceptual presentation, but which I nevertheless perceive, such as "objects behind my back."

2) The experience of imagining absences, possibilities, potentialities, contingencies, counter-factual conditionals, the subjunctive, the optative, etc.

3) The perception of others insofar as the perception of the other presents a body (surface) in which there is a (non-spatial) mind, the body being "visible," the mind being "invisible" (in the sense of the Husserlian appresented object). The experience of my own mind in my own body which is "posterior" to the experience of embodiment.

4) The silence which surrounds language, as *la langue* "precedes" and surrounds *la parole*.

5) Consciousness and Unconsciousness.

6) The Husserlian distinction between fact and essence.

7) The relationship between the present state of a science which is moving towards a more perfect stage of the same science, which will be recognizably the *same*-science, though it does not yet exist. Etc. See above, Chapter 3.

18. *Ibid.*, pp. 125-126.

INDEX OF NAMES

INDEX OF TOPICS

φ

3279

AB

N73HPB

EDIE